Blessings

an autobiographical fragment

Books by Mary Craig

LONGFORD
WOODRUFF AT RANDOM (ed.) (Associated Catholic Publications)

Blessings

an autobiographical fragment

by

Mary Craig

HODDER AND STOUGHTON
LONDON SYDNEY AUCKLAND TORONTO

British Library Cataloguing in Publication Data

Craig, Mary
  Blessings.
  1. Craig, Mary 2. Social workers –
  Great Britain – Biography
  1 Title
  361'.92'4   HV28.C/

  ISBN 0 340 23561 6

First published 1979

Copyright © 1979 by Mary Craig

*Printed in Great Britain for
Hodder and Stoughton Ltd.,
Mill Road, Dunton Green, Sevenoaks, Kent
by Ebenezer Baylis & Son Ltd.,
The Trinity Press, Worcester, and London.*

The life that I have is all that I have,
    The life that I have is yours.

The love that I have of the life that I have,
    Is yours and yours and yours.

A sleep I shall have, a rest I shall have,
    Yet death will be but a pause.

For the peace of my years in the long green grass
    Will be yours and yours and yours.

Code poem used by Violette Szabo, the British resistance heroine who worked in France and was shot at Ravensbrück Concentration Camp.

For Anthony and Mark,
who will read and understand.
And for Nicholas who will not.

Acknowledgments

James Walsh S.J., editor of *The Way*, for permission to draw on an article I wrote for the January 1973 issue; and the Rev. Canon Michael Mayne of the BBC Religious Broadcasting Department, who made me re-think the material for a Lent Talk on radio (Bare Essentials, March 1977, BBC Radio 4)

Elizabeth Longford, Morris West and David Winter, who read and approved the MS with an enthusiasm which surpassed my wildest hopes.

John Harriott, without whose encouragement I should never have begun to write, on this or any other subject; and Edward England of Hodders who, having read the article in *The Way*, insisted on my writing this particular book.

Pat and Jessica, my much-loved friends, who checked my reminiscences of Cavendish and found them authentic; Sue Ryder (now Baroness Ryder) for the special inspiration she has always provided; and 'the Bods' themselves, in whose debt I shall always remain.

Betty, for what she has given all of us, but especially for her devotion to Paul and Nicholas.

And Frank, whose story this is as much as it is mine, and who has had much to endure.

Cold Ash, Newbury, June 1978.

Contents

1 'You Know He Isn't Normal . . .'   page 13

2 Paul   24

3 Despair   34

4 Cavendish   39

5 Paul Goes to Poland   51

6 Nicholas   59

7 Breaking the Shell   65

8 Journey to Poland   69

9 Sue, Paul and a Party   77

10 Wanda, Hanka and Others   83

11 The End of the Journey   89

12 A Death in the Family   98

13 A Year-round Christmas Gift   105

14 What Makes the Desert Beautiful . . .   118

CHAPTER I

'You Know He Isn't Normal . . .'

IN 1956 THERE were three of us: Frank, my husband, an industrial chemist whom I had met when we were both undergraduates at Oxford, Anthony, our year-old son and myself. We had just had a house built in a village a few miles outside of Derby, but we did not really belong to that part of the country, and the Midlands never felt like home. Home for Frank was Hampshire, whereas I had sprung from the smoke and soot of St Helens, a grey town in what was then called Lancashire. Nowadays it has been renamed Merseyside, much to the disgust of its inhabitants.

We spent quite a lot of time in St Helens, since my widowed mother lived there, and it was not such a very long haul from Derby in our tinny second-hand Morris Eight. Whenever we went there, a little spastic girl who lived lower down the road used to come in and play with Anthony. She was a nice child, very gentle and affectionate, and really very intelligent. But she filled me with horror simply because she was not normal, and I hated abnormality of any kind. I despised myself for it, but every time that Margaret came to my mother's house, a wave of revulsion swept over me. I could not bear to see this malformed and inarticulate child play with my son; and I wished with all my heart that she would stay away.

Where we lived in Derbyshire we had no Catholic church, but attended Mass every Sunday in a hired room above a local pub. Among the fairly small congregation was a woman who came along each week with her three tall sons. I no longer remember the names of the other two, but the middle one, I know, was called John, and he was mentally handicapped. After Mass, the mother always made a fuss of this boy, taking his arm lovingly on the way home. Could she not see how repulsive he was? Did she, I wondered, see him as he really was, or were mothers of such children blinded by mother-love?

Like most people, I suppose, I was frightened by my rare encounters with the unthinkable. I cherished the belief that abnormality was something that happened to others. It couldn't possibly happen to me. But it did.

My second pregnancy was unremarkable, except that I was sick rather a lot, and was unusually nervy and irrational. (On the day when two gipsy-women had called at the house selling clothes-pegs and heather, Frank found me sitting under the stairs, terrified to death, when he came home from work.) For the birth itself I went over to St Helens, where I had booked an amenity bed in a small teaching-hospital near my mother's home. The night that I went into labour, I remember speaking to a friend on the telephone, and telling her that I was scared stiff, much more frightened than I had been the first time. And it wasn't really the pain that I was afraid of; there was a deeper, free-floating anxiety which I was at a loss to explain.

It was, in fact, a very difficult labour, followed by a high forceps delivery and a breech birth. I lost an inordinate amount of blood, and afterwards felt exhausted and ill, with none of the elation which I had felt when Anthony was born. The baby, another boy, was large, about 8lbs 12ozs, and when they showed him to me, declaring that he was beautiful, I shivered. Flesh seemed to droop off him, like an overcoat several sizes too large. To my own dismay, I felt no urge to take him in my arms or cuddle him. Instead I found myself turning away.

But as the days passed the initial feeling of revulsion passed too. I stopped noticing that he looked odd, or perhaps I decided that the oddness was all in my imagination. The nurses seemed genuinely enthusiastic about him, so I began taking my cue from them.

The trouble really began when I took him home, to my mother's, and tried to feed him myself, as I had done with Anthony enjoyably enough. He was insatiable, and although I had plenty of milk I was soon making up a bottle for him as well. First half-strength, then full-strength. It didn't matter how much I gave him, he went on crying and looking for more. In the end I gave up trying to breast-feed and put him onto extra-strength powdered milk. Not that it made much difference, but it was less exhausting for me. In retrospect it seems to me that he didn't stop crying for the next five years or so, but I suppose memory is playing me false. He *must* have slept sometimes.

We called him Paul Christopher. Friends assured us that once he had passed his first birthday he was bound to improve; and we waited longingly for that scarcely-to-be-believed-in day. Meanwhile he cried so long and so hard that he ruptured himself. He was only ten weeks old when our doctor discovered a hernia and decided that an immediate operation was called for. In a way, in spite of our obvious anxiety, the crisis was something of a relief. We thought that perhaps the mystery of his crying had been solved: he had had the hernia all the time without our suspecting it. Now perhaps he would stop crying. But the crisis came and went. Paul came out of hospital crying as hard as ever.

All that crying did not seem to affect his growth, and he was putting on weight fast. The sagging pockets of flesh were filling out, and in the foolish way that parents have we rather gloated over the phenomenal growth-rate. He was well ahead of the other babies at the local clinic, tipping the scales at a rate that caused eyebrows to rise. My mother-in-law spiked our complacency by hinting that this might be a cause for alarm rather than pride, but though we were both irritated by her seeming lack of perception we did not let it worry us for long.

Paul's first birthday arrived, that magic day when the crying was to stop and peace be restored. Alas for our hope. On that day he excelled himself, bawling for the entire day and reducing us all to a frazzle. So much for the prophecies of our friends; we should have to go on waiting.

Memories become blurred. At some time during the year that followed, I suppose he must have improved, because I remember a brief happy period when he was large and cheerful, with big china-blue eyes and masses of golden curls. An attractive child, mistaken by almost everyone for a girl. But our friends were even then beginning to be uneasy; they were noticing what we were too close to see: that Paul's blue eyes lacked intelligence, his nose was without a bridge, and the fingers on his chubby hands were disconcertingly spatula-shaped. He had done most of the expected things at the normal time – sitting up, cutting teeth, crawling, but one thing he had not yet done was talk. Instead of talking he made bizarre noises, rough, meaningless sounds which could not possibly be mistaken for speech. Unwittingly we joked about it. Anthony by this time was very advanced for his age and was bursting to go to school. Paul, we laughed, without any sense of foreboding, was certain to grace the bottom end of the class rather than the top. Perhaps he'd be good at football instead. A visiting social worker hinted that he might be deaf and suggested a hearing-test. But deafness was an unthinkable stigma, and I would not entertain the possibility of it.

About three months before Paul was two, I discovered, to my horror, that I was pregnant again. After the last experience, I could hardly welcome the prospect of another baby, but as I would not have considered having an abortion I had to get used to the idea. I was worried, though. With a restless three-year-old Anthony, and with Paul, my hands and days were completely full. And as if to underline the awkwardness of my new state, a few days later Paul was once again whipped off into hospital – again with a strangulating hernia.

In 1957 we had moved from Derbyshire to Hale, in Cheshire, which was much nearer to St Helens. Packing Anthony off to his grandmother's, I was free to visit the hospital as often as I was allowed. But though I went down there each day, nobody was able to tell me what the programme was likely to be. Paul had a wheezy chest, and as long as this was in evidence, it was not likely that he would be given an anaesthetic. It began to look as though he would be sent home untouched by medical hand, strangulating hernia or not.

The night when everything fell apart was a Tuesday in February, 1958, and every detail is etched like poker-work into my mind. The previous evening, the Sister in charge of the children's ward had asked if I would come early, as the house doctor would like a word with me. Somehow I presumed that the operation must be off, and I would be asked to bring Paul in each day as an out-patient.

Frank, who at this time was a manager with the Associated Octel Company in Northwich, was bringing a French colleague home to dinner, and fitting in the 6.30 visit to the hospital was a bit difficult. I had a mad scurry round before leaving, and at six o'clock put some sort of casserole into the oven. When I came back I should have to serve the meal immediately, and I wasn't taking any chances. No instinct told me, as I closed the front door and stepped out into the chill February night, that the door was closing on everything I had been: that this night would mark a new and fearful beginning. It seemed a night like any other, except that I was worrying about the dinner-guest.

When I got to the hospital, I didn't go to the ward, but asked the girl at the reception-desk to tell the house-doctor that I had arrived. I was directed into a small waiting-room on the ground-floor. Within a few minutes a white-coated doctor walked in, a sheaf of papers in his hand. He was a man of about thirty or so, recently arrived from some Middle Eastern country, with no more than a sketchy idea of the English language, and none at all of the language of diplomacy.

'You are the mother of . . . -er, -er . . .' He rifled idly through the papers in his hand. 'Ah, yes, Paul Craig?' I nodded.

'Of course, you know he is not normal,' he continued, in the same tone as before. His voice didn't ask a question, it made a statement.

NOT NORMAL. I stared at him blankly, my world slowly dissolving, all reality crystallising into that one murderous phrase

2

which a stranger had just uttered with such casual ease. Not normal, not normal. My mind struggled with this alien concept, but could not grasp it. I felt buffeted by meaningless words which were heavy with menace. The voice went on, as though the world was still the same; it was a voice that struggled with a language that wasn't its own; a voice that lacked warmth and understanding. 'He has Höhler's Syndrome, a rare disease. In English you call it . . . -er, gargoylism.'

Through the thickening fog in my head I heard him, and into my punch-drunk consciousness swam hideous figures, straight off the pages of *Notre Dame de Paris* — gargoyles. Monstrous creatures carved in stone, water gushing out of their leering mouths. Oh God, not that; anything but that. Not my son.

Like a drunk crazily determined to walk a straight line if it kills him, I managed to dredge up some words. Very slowly, and as though from an immense distance, I heard my own voice ask the question which was already tormenting me. 'Will he be all right? I mean . . . his mind. Mentally?' I can still see that doctor shrug away the question. It was more than his scanty English could cope with — and in any case, there was no answer. 'I do not know. You must wait and see,' he said impatiently. And walked out.

It seemed like hours that I sat there after he had gone, not even trying to collect my scattering wits. Then in a drug-like stupor I dragged myself to the telephone and rang Frank. I don't think I did more than ask him to come for me. I wouldn't have found words to tell him what had happened.

In a trance I walked up the stairs to the children's ward, where I sat looking at Paul, with a heavy boulder where my heart had been. The scales fell from my eyes then with brutal suddenness. Self-deception was no longer possible; and I could see beyond doubting that Paul would never be as other children were. The stubby fingers, the too-thick lips, the flattened, bridge-less nose, the empty eyes, all pointed to this hateful but inescapable truth which we had gone on hiding from ourselves.

Frank came and took me home. It must have been terrible for him, but I was overwhelmed by my own misery and had no room for his. We had to go through the farce of a dinner-party, since our guest was a Frenchman who had nowhere else to go while waiting for his return flight from Ringway Airport, which was about five miles from where we lived. He knew something awful had happened, but we couldn't trust ourselves to talk about it. There was a spectre at that feast, and both the food and the effort at conversation nearly choked us.

When he had gone, we packed a suitcase apiece, and drove silently to my mother's. She had alerted her own doctor, an old family friend, and he had left a sedative for me. I took it with relief. It was a new product, which was just finding its way onto the market, and, because it was effective that first night and was easily available over the counter in chemists' shops, Frank went and bought a new supply of tablets for me next day. I went on taking them for several weeks. It was not until nearly two years later that the name of this product, Distaval, came into a shocking prominence, as one of the names for thalidomide. I was two months' pregnant and I took the tablets for at least a month. My blood runs cold at the thought of our narrow escape on this occasion: Mark, the child born in the December of that year, was a perfect baby.

There is a mental blank where the next few weeks must have been. All I remember is that after the first night I could shed no tears; a great freeze had descended on my emotional system. I was not, as some people believed, 'being wonderfully brave'; I was merely in an extended state of shock, with all my capacity for feeling paralysed. Perhaps it was nature's own kind of anaesthetic.

What triggered the change I don't remember, but I can never forget the night when the anaesthesia wore off, and I was left to wrestle with my blinding, asphyxiating terrors in a foretaste of hell. Despair rolled through me in waves as I looked into the future I did not want to face, and found it full of grotesque images: of enlarged heads, swollen abdomens and drooling mouths. The dreadful word 'gargoyle' was working its evil in me, filling me with self-pity and panic. From now on, I felt sure, I would see myself and be seen as some kind of pariah, the mother of a monstrous child. Friends would avoid me, and Paul would be

taken away. Oddly enough, in view of all this self-pity, the fear
of Paul's being dragged off to an institution was the blackest one
of all. However agonising it might be to look after him, I could
not face the prospect of letting him go.

It was the mother of an old school-friend who brought some
sanity into my exhausted brain. 'Look,' she said briskly, 'if you
ever do come to send him away, you and Frank will have arrived at
the decision yourselves. No-one is going to drag Paul away screaming. For Heaven's sake, stop worrying about something that may
never happen!' I knew she was right, and tried to cheer up. As I
got up to leave, she came out with one of those pious clichés
which at certain moments have tremendous force. 'God makes the
back for the burden,' she offered, by way of consolation. The
phrase impressed me, simply because it seemed so unlikely. God
had picked a loser this time, one whose back was near to breaking
under the strain.

Frank and I were both Catholics, conventional enough without
being particularly enthusiastic. It didn't bother us much one way
or the other, and at this stage it would not have occurred to us to
look for any comfort in God or our Catholic faith. But to the
Lancashire Catholics among whom I grew up (especially those
of my mother's generation) life was nothing if not religion, and
there were conventional pieties to cover almost any contingency.
When things went wrong, God would put them right, though
it must be admitted that, in their experience, he had very rarely
done so. Nothing troubled their faith that God was a kind and
loving Father; and doubt was alien to them, a shameful thing. My
mother, I am quite sure, had never allowed even a momentary
doubt to cloud her faith. Her own life had contained almost an
unfair share of tragedy — she too had had a handicapped son, her
husband had died of killer pneumonia at the age of thirty-two,
and as his body was brought from their home in Scotland by
train to Leeds for burial in the family vault, her young son had
fallen from the train and been killed. Father and son were buried
on the same day, while she was six months' pregnant with her
second child, myself. When the time came for me to be born, she
had quite plainly decided that she would die, because she left

instructions that I was to be called Dolorosa, 'child of grief'. (I had another narrow escape there.) But that was her only concession to despair, and she never doubted that God was a loving God. Still less did she doubt His existence. My mother went every morning to Mass, and was never happier than when she was in church. Religion was not only a consolation, it was her talisman against life. Say the right prayers, make the right Novena, speak to the right saint, and all would be well. It was a child-like, untroubled faith, shared by many of her friends; and though on many occasions it reduced me to fury, I think now that such calm certainty is to be envied.

When an uncle in Dublin offered to pay all expenses if we wanted to take Paul to Lourdes, my mother was sure that her prayers had been answered. She genuinely believed that it was only a matter of time before Paul would be cured, and she urged us to accept my uncle's offer with all speed. We, of course, were much less sanguine, but, for reasons which were not the same as my mother's, we decided that we would go to Lourdes with Paul. We saw it as a gesture of sorts, and some kind of gesture seemed to be called for. Some symbolic act which would underline the separation of past from future. Besides, though neither of us came within a million miles of my mother's faith, we did believe that Lourdes had something to offer us. It was not the spring-water or the hope of miracles which drew us, but the feeling that in such a place we might be able to put our own problem in perspective. If nothing else, we would have visible proof that we were not alone.

There is in fact no better cure for self-pity than Lourdes. Where the sick and the maimed seem to pour together to proclaim their hope and their faith, or even just to share their fears, it is no longer possible to believe that one's own pain is either unique or unbearable. The discovery holds at least a measure of comfort.

We pushed, pulled and heaved Paul in a wheel-chair up, down and around, missing nothing. We went to the torchlight procession in the evening, and as a matter of course joined the massive crowds in the afternoon for the ritual blessing of the sick. It had not occurred to me to ask if I could join the group of mothers of sick children who were in a special reserved area at the front, near the altar, and generally Frank and I, with Paul, were somewhere in the middle of the heaving throng. One afternoon we had gone there as usual, and, as the priest came by, the sacred monstrance raised in his hands for blessing, the crowd fell silent. And in that pin-dropping silence Paul began to laugh. It was the laugh of a mad creature, a spine-chilling cackle that froze me to the spot with horror and shame. Suddenly an old peasant woman in a black shawl elbowed her way to where we stood and, eyes streaming with tears, lifted Paul out of his wheel-chair and held him up in her arms for the priest to bless. Paul was so astonished that he stopped laughing. It was an agonised moment, the significance of which did not escape me even at the time. It was another woman who had wept for my child, and who had taken compassion on me. Instinctively she had done what the moment demanded.

The woman's action pulled me up short. From that moment I shook myself out of my stupor, and scraped together some scraps of courage. I can't claim to have been inspired by anything more noble than common-sense and the urge to self-preservation, but they were enough for a start. The alternatives stared me in the face: either I could go on wallowing, over-protecting myself from hurt, becoming more and more bitter each day as I played the insidious chorus of 'why-should-this-happen-to-me?' as the background music to my life. Or — I could face the fact that what had happened was not going to un-happen, and might as well be come to terms with. I had been drowning in self-pity for long enough now to see where it was likely to lead. There was no doubt in my mind that I needed to change course.

Anyway, I was beginning to look forward to the new baby. A number of people had expressed horror – 'Surely you're not going on with it?' Relatives and friends were full of forebodings and fears, but somehow I knew with absolute certainty that their fears would be confounded. The new baby would be a consolation, not a fresh disaster. For once I was right. The birth was easy; the child, John Mark, everything I could have hoped for. With Paul at home, and Anthony a restless, energetic four-year-old, the new baby had to be propped up with a bottle and left to get on with it. He seemed to know from the start that he couldn't expect anything better, and to the relief of us all, he seemed to thrive on the inevitable neglect.

CHAPTER 2

Paul

DURING THE FIRST four years of Paul's life, there was little relief. A local girl, Jean (who became a lifelong and invaluable friend), came in once a week to help with the cleaning; but, except that I went shopping when she was there, I was almost completely housebound and Paul-bound. Frank and I had no social life. In those four years, at least, we never went out in the evenings. Dinner-parties, theatres, cinemas, were things once known but long-forgotten.

Once I had thought of myself as a woman with intellectual interests, but now my life was focused entirely on Paul. The other children too, of course, but mainly Paul. There was so much to do for him. Doubly incontinent, he was always having to be changed or cleaned up; he had to be watched constantly because his actions were unpredictable; and he had to be fed, like a baby, by hand, every spoonful shovelled into his mouth, since he could hold neither spoon nor cup for himself. And as he would chew everything a hundred times over, with maddening slowness, the time for getting the next meal ready was almost in sight by the time he'd got to the end of the previous one. He was a round-the-clock full-time job.

When I look back now on those early years with Paul, they

float in a mist of unreality. Can I really have got up two, three, four times every night to put him back to bed when he was chasing round and round his room like one possessed? I know that I did, and I remember thinking hopelessly that it would never end, that I'd go on doing that for ever and ever, or until the accumulating exhaustion got me down. Paul wouldn't even have a rest in the middle of the day to make up for the sleep he lost at night. He seemed never to get tired.

At first, I think it was other people from whom we suffered most, because it takes time to learn how not to mind, and you have to work at it. 'Old fish-face', the children in the road called after us, when I took him out in his pram. Paul didn't hear, and if he had heard he would not have understood, so why should I mind so much? I don't know, but I did. Sometimes the children just ran away when they saw us coming, and I had to steel myself to pretend that I hadn't noticed that the street was suddenly empty. Once I took Paul on a bus into nearby Altrincham, and I froze when I heard a woman behind me say: 'Children like that shouldn't be allowed on public transport. It's not right.' At that moment, I remembered, with a sharp stab of anguish, how I had felt about poor spastic Margaret.

I'm sure that it's fear which deprives well-intentioned people of their normal sensitivity. Or it may be that the shock of horror is so strong as to oust all other, more generous, feelings. Whatever the reason, I seemed to spend my life nerving myself against the barbs of those who certainly meant no harm, but who couldn't have hurt more if they had put their minds to it. There was a doctor, for example, an old family friend, who passed me by in the street one morning without a word, and with barely a nod of recognition. Next day he came round to the house sweating with outrage. 'An animal,' he almost shouted at me, 'that's what he is, an animal. Why don't you have him put away?' He was working something out of his system, and he didn't seem to realise what his words were doing to me.

Poor Paul, so gentle he would never consciously have hurt anything or anybody, but so clumsy that he couldn't help doing so. He infuriated Anthony. The latter was keen on making models of ships and aeroplanes, but there was no way in which the finished models could be kept safe from Paul's marauding hands. He would trample on the other children's toys and chew the wheels off their miniature motor-cars. Worse, he swallowed not only the rubber tyres, but every nut, bolt and screw he could lay hands on. We worried constantly, but the strange diet didn't seem to affect his health.

Sometimes he played in the garden, usually in a small glossy red car, which was his pride and joy. He went on shunting himself around in it, even when he had long since outgrown it. Cars were his great love, and he was always happy when he was in one. Going for a ride in our elderly Ford Consul used to exhilarate him, and he would sit bolt upright on the back seat, with a seraphic grin plastered all over his face. He regarded everything that happened in the car as entertainment laid on specially for his benefit. Once Frank inadvertently backed into a lamp-post and swore colourfully. Paul thought it was a marvellous joke, and rocked with an appreciative belly-laugh which didn't improve his father's temper.

We both did what we could for him, but sadly there was no question of a loving relationship between us. For love you need some kind of basic communication, a reciprocity. With Paul there was nothing. If he knew us at all, it was only as a vaguely friendly presence; there was no real recognition in his awareness of us.

Try as we would, we could never teach him that some things are just not done. He was incapable of learning from his frequent mistakes. If he pulled out the cutlery drawer from its moorings and proceeded to hurl its contents on to the floor, as he regularly did, you could give him a smack and put back the knives and forks a thousand times, but he never related the smack to what he had done. Cause and effect had no meaning for him; and neither had right and wrong; or dangerous and not-dangerous. In the end it seemed safer to limit him to one room, away from any obvious danger, with a few comparatively harmless toys to play with.

I still shudder when I recall the endless visits to hospital clinics, the hours of waiting for the ambulance 'milk-round', the countless requests from medical practitioners of varying eminence who all wanted permission to view this child with the rare and fascinating text-book disease. So rare that few of the doctors had come across it before; and they were eager to remedy the deficiency. 'There are so few of these cases around,' they would explain eagerly, bursting with professional excitement. 'If you let us examine Paul, you will be making your contribution to scientific research into his disease.' So Paul and I trudged (I didn't drive in those days) to one clinic after another, meeting students who stood in awed or bored astonishment, while their tutors prodded and poked and pointed out Paul's salient symptoms, referring to me throughout as 'the mother', as though I were not actually present in the room at all. Paul would play to the gallery on these occasions, acting the circus clown; while I sat there, positively crunching my teeth and reminding myself at intervals not to get sour.

When Paul was about four, I met a Belgian professor from Louvain who offered to try and cure him. Research on the subject of Höhler's Syndrome was more advanced on the continent than in Britain, and it was this man's speciality.

It was the first time we had been given any hope. Full of excitement, we decided to take Paul to Louvain. We didn't have a particularly auspicious beginning; for some reason we decided it would be better to fly from Heathrow rather than from Ringway, which was near our home. But by the time we arrived at Heathrow, fog had grounded the planes at every airport in the country — except Ringway. We had a nightmarish wait of nine hours, in the airport lounge with an increasingly ebullient and noisy Paul.

When we eventually arrived at the Clinique St Raphaël, where Paul was to be investigated, we found that specialists from all over Belgium were coming to see him; radiologists, ENT surgeons, neurologists, pathologists and cardiac consultants. One neurologist we met was quite excited. This man had written a medical tract on 'la pathogénie du gargoylisme', and was regarded as an international authority on the subject. He took me on one side to tell me about the little girl he had once treated, who had been completely paralysed by the disease. When given the treatment he had recommended, she was able to sit up and play with her toys, feed herself and even run about. Paul, he assured us, was in far better shape than this other child had been. In fact, Paul was the 'best' case of gargoylism he had ever seen; and he had every confidence that a cure could be found for him. I could hardly contain my own excitement.

Frank had come over to Louvain with us, but he had had to return to work in England at the end of the week. So after that time I was in constant attendance on Paul, who did not like Louvain or any of the things that were happening to him there. He hated and feared all the tests, blood-counts, injections, throat-swabs etc, and he refused to drink any of the concoctions he was offered so enticingly. His fears boiled over one morning when he was summoned for a cardiograph. He kicked, fought and bit the poor young nurse who was vainly attempting to hold him still. Mysteriously, sedatives only served to excite him and make him more uncontrollable than ever. There was nothing for it but to bring in reinforcements; in the end, six people held down the struggling Paul, one on each limb and one on each end. He fought like a fury, but he could not win. He cheered up later on though, when he went to have his photograph taken: he loved the electronic flashes, and wanted more.

On arrival at the hospital, I had been asked if I would mind taking Paul along one day to meet a few students. No, I said, of course I didn't mind. The presence of half-a-dozen or so students every time Paul was examined was by now a commonplace of life. A few more would make no difference.

So, early one morning, an escort came for Paul and myself. We were led down endless corridors, and across a quadrangle into another building, where we were ushered through a small door — straight onto the stage of a lecture theatre. I almost reeled with the shock of it, for, crowding the theatre in their serried ranks were the 'few' students who had been invited to see Paul — about five hundred of them. I suspect that the professors had issued a three-line Whip to get them there!

I sat there mute and choking, while Paul, hyper-excited by the tension and the spotlight so obviously focused on him, played up, charging round in concentric circles, and laughing his zany idiot laugh. With clinical detachment the lecturer began to point out the tell-tale signs. 'Observe this child,' he invited his audience. 'The spatulate hands are typical of Höhler's Syndrome. Notice too the protruding abdomen, the curvature of the spine . . .' On and on he went; and Paul gurgled and lurched around, paying his unwitting dues to science. I forced myself to stay seated, to stay calm, when every instinct in me wanted to run and run, far from that terrible place. 'They need to know all they can find out about this disease,' I told myself sternly, 'so they need Paul. It's in the interests of science.' Science, science, what the hell did I care about science? They could have pinned a Nobel medal for services to medical knowledge to my chest, and I should not have cared. All I wanted was to be a thousand miles away from that vast concourse of young people, to whom I was being indifferently pointed out as 'the mother' of a monstrous son. It was my moment of utter humiliation and abandonment; and it left a scar which has never healed.

It was all in vain, anyway. All our hopes came to nothing. But when I left the Clinique St Raphaël I didn't know that. The doctors permitted themselves a cautious optimism. Paul, they had concluded, was suffering from over-stimulation of the pituitary gland, and they had a suitable treatment worked out. It would involve some risky radiation therapy, but it just might work.

There was nothing either cautious or qualified about my own reaction to the verdict. Disregarding the enormous ifs and buts which hedged it round, I soared from despair to riotous hope. Floating on air, after my final interview with the eminent professor H., I dashed upstairs to the room I shared with Paul and recorded in my diary, with a naïveté which makes me blush to re-read it, 'Wonderful, wonderful news. We are going to see Paul improving in every respect, growing slimmer and taller, with finer features, better hearing, less excitability, more responsiveness. In fact, it sounds as though within five or six months we shan't recognise him.' Poor silly fool, I had heard only what I wanted to hear, and had entirely missed the crucial point that the achievement of this miracle was no more than an odds-on chance. With near-manic enthusiasm, I was busy planning Paul's future, doubtless speculating on whether he would go to Oxford or Cambridge.

Back home in Hale, a little more cold realism took over. The treatment recommended, irradiation of the tiny pituitary gland, situated at the base of the brain, was a tricky one and virtually unknown in Britain. It could not be undertaken lightly, on the say-so of a European doctor, however pre-eminent in his specialist field. But we were fortunate to have the Christie Hospital and Holt Radium Institute nearby in Manchester, and the doctors there agreed to give the treatment a trial on the National Health system. But they warned us that the risks were great, and they were ours alone. We asked them to go ahead.

And so, except when Frank could be free to take us by car, Paul and I started the ambulance milk-round again. Whole days were swallowed up in endless waiting – for the ambulance to come, for other patients who had to be collected en route, for the doctor to arrive, for the treatment to be given, for the anaesthetic to wear off, for the ambulance to return. Six hours was what it usually took, each week, with hope slowly dwindling to vanishing-point as Paul's condition did not alter. After a few months of this, when there was not the faintest sign of improvement, the doctors were unwilling to subject Paul to further radiation. Reluctantly we had to face the fact that there had been no cure, no improvement, but possibly some deterioration. It is a fact that Paul lost the one phrase he had so far been able to master. After the treatment, we never again heard him say – 'Bye-bye'.

Life with Paul went on being traumatic, but by 1960 there was a welcome relief. My mother and my Aunt Betty both retired, my mother very unwillingly from her job as a much revered local headmistress, and President of most of the teachers' and head teachers' organisations in St Helens; my aunt much more enthusiastically from a strenuous post in industrial nursing. Both were now free, with time on their hands and plenty of energy to expend. They decided that I ought to be the main beneficiary, and were very anxious to help.

Betty was the practical one, and she was wonderful with Paul. She had no illusions about what he could or could not do, and she knew he would never be any different. She simply accepted him as he was and did everything in her power to make his life a happy one. My mother was good with him too, but she had never come to terms with the situation. She had taken refuge in a sort of fantasy world in which Paul was no more than 'delicate'; and she was quite happy with this version of the truth. Her own first child, my brother Tony, had been, as far as we were able to make out, very like Paul, but my mother had never accepted the truth about him either. He had died before I was born, and in my early years my mother constantly told me how good Tony was, how helpful, even how clever. Her fantasy even extended to the manner of his death. He had died, she said, of appendicitis. It was left to others to tell me that he had been severely sub-normal, and that he had been killed when falling out of a train. The various doctors who made a study of Paul and who asked about my family history, got no change out of my mother. I could tell them the little I knew or suspected, but it didn't amount to much. *She* would admit nothing.

Betty — or Beb — as the children have always called her — was not my aunt at all, or indeed any relation. She was the nursing-sister in charge of the maternity ward where I was born. My mother had gone into the hospital to await my arrival and what she hoped would be her own demise. Betty had sympathised, taken special care of her, and afterwards had come to visit her at home. She was glad to make a friend, since her own home was in Yorkshire, and she had only just come to St Helens. Years later, when Betty decided to leave hospital work and take a job in industry, she moved in with us as a temporary arrangement — and stayed. We were a rather fearsomely all-female household: my mother, Gertrude, the sister with whom she had gone to live when my father died, Betty and myself. (The only men who ever came near were an occasional uncle and the parish priest.) I was always fond of Betty and was closer to her than to my mother. She and I would talk and share secrets, something I never did with my mother, of whom I was always in awe. The discovery, when I was ten or so, that Betty was not a blood-relation, was one of the most miserable moments of my childhood. I felt betrayed.

My mother had not even told Betty the truth about her son, Tony: she too had been told how clever he was. Then one day she met an old doctor who asked her if she had known my mother when Tony was alive. She said she hadn't. 'It was such a mercy he died,' the old man said, 'he would have been a millstone around his mother's neck.' But when Betty reported this strange conversation, my mother refuted it hotly. She had quite convinced herself of Tony's normality.

So it was quite logical that she would see the Paul-situation through the same rose-tinted spectacles: she could not bear very much reality. But she loved Paul, and though she could not do for him what Betty could, she did her best. After their retirement, they both became frequent visitors to our house, though it was Betty who came more often. Betty, in fact, had offered to come for three days each week to look after Paul while I took a part-time job. The Headmistress of the school where Anthony was now in the kindergarten had asked if I could come and teach Latin in the senior school, and with Betty's heroic help I should be able to. It wasn't the teaching in itself that was so attractive. It was the opportunity it presented of escaping at least for a few hours from my own four walls. It was a way of preserving my sanity. Thank God for Betty.

CHAPTER 3

Despair

PAUL WAS GETTING on for five and in the normal way of things would have been going to school. One of the tortures inflicted on parents of mentally-handicapped children at that time was the ordeal by letter. A school doctor was sent to the house to investigate the child's suitability for normal schooling (in spite of his or her very obvious non-suitability), and then would follow a formal letter, stating explicitly that the child was sub-normal and therefore unable to benefit from normal education (the word they used was 'ineducable'). Everybody concerned was well aware of this fact before the process was set in motion, but for some reason it had to be spelled out, the i's dotted, the t's crossed, and the parents' noses thoroughly rubbed in the dirt. Most parents resented this official humiliation, but they could do nothing about it. When our turn came, and I was told to expect the arrival of a school doctor, I bowed to the inevitable. It was only a routine visit after all.

But it did not turn out quite as expected. I have often hoped that the school doctor who came to see Paul that day was not typical of her species. There she stood on the doorstep, a large, bouncy, tweedy woman whose burly torso positively heaved with excitement. We had not met before, but she absolved herself from the courtesy of introductions. I had barely got the front door open before she announced with breathless fervour: 'I can't wait to see this child. Do you think he might possibly be a cretin?'

Blind rage swept over me, and I would have given much to slam the door, or, better still, my clenched fist, in her jolly face. How does it happen that doctors, who presumably set out on their careers because they see themselves as healers, become so frequently insensitive to other people's pain? For years Paul and I were no more than objects to be examined under a microscope, two animate creatures of momentary interest to medicine. It never seemed to occur to anyone, or if it did it did not seem to matter, that we were also sentient human beings who could be badly hurt. It was difficult learning to be a non-person, but I was learning fast. Building up a hard shell within which to shelter was part of the process of learning. The only sure way to protect myself from hurt was by refusing to be hurt at all, refusing to notice, refusing to care. Ordinary human feelings were becoming a luxury I could not afford.

That doctor had almost penetrated my defences, but my public self-control was still armour-plated. So I forced a smile and asked her in, and we began, as one inevitably did, on the old, old questions. Who is he, what is he, why is he, when, how, where? The questions rolled off an endless cyclic conveyor belt, and were answered as mechanically as they were asked. If I had been better organised, I should have made out a list of questions and answers, and made photostats of them to hand out. They were always the same. We always began at the beginning, at pregnancy if not at conception, and worked right through. No-one ever came pre-armed with the relevant facts, there had never been any liaison with previous questioners (even when they came from the same hospital or local authority), no data bank of information was ever consulted, if indeed any existed. We always started with a *tabula rasa*. The game began on square one, and our opponents were always the victors, if one could judge by the flushed face and air of triumph they wore on departure.

Even with Betty's help, the strain was beginning to tell. I was getting to the end of my resources. The climax came one day when

I was alone in the house with Paul. I went into the room where he was playing and found that not only had he soiled himself, but he was cheerfully smearing the faeces all over the wall. Ours was a largish Edwardian house, with half-landings recessed into a sweeping staircase. Holding Paul under the armpits I began to drag him up the stairs towards the bathroom, paying no attention to his squawks of protest. We had reached the first half-landing when he began to cough. I stopped there, but the coughing fit grew worse. Suddenly, to my horror, his breathing became jerky, he began to choke, and his face went black. I was terrified, stuck as I was half-way up the stairs and nobody within earshot. With a strength born of desperation, I pushed and pulled him up the remaining stairs and inside the bathroom. Shutting the door on him, I fled downstairs to the telephone to order an ambulance. Then I rushed madly up again to try and get him cleaned up.

The ambulance came. Unfortunately, in my panic, I had given no details over the telephone. I had omitted to say that Paul was breathing only with difficulty; and the ambulance arrived without the vital cylinder of oxygen. The minutes seemed like hours as we waited for the second ambulance to arrive, and Paul's condition got worse with every breath he tried to take.

The oxygen arrived in the nick of time, and Paul was taken off to hospital to recover from the first of many bronchial convulsions. He came out within a week, fully restored and entirely cheerful. But my nerves were raw. The problem of Paul had me utterly beat.

In the summer of 1962, we took the family to the seaside.
But I could not relax; the change of environment only made me
more conscious that I had come to the end of the road in more
ways than one. I had lost sight of myself as a person, I viewed
the future with fear, and I realised with a shock that even my
rather vague religion had deserted me. I no longer believed in
God. What more was there to lose? Self-pity, always lurking in
the background, came surging in on a flood-tide. Life was absurd
and meaningless, was it not, a dirty-tricks department writ large?
And the whole idea of a loving God was a hollow sham, a cosmic
joke worthy only of Paul's crazy laughter. But there was no way
out of the impasse, and I could only go on compounding the
meaninglessness. Suicide, even if I had not been the devout coward
I in fact was, would only have shifted the whole ghastly mess into
someone else's court, and I was not far enough gone to accept
that as an answer.

Frank suggested that I should go away on my own for a week.
I jumped at the idea, but couldn't think where to go. I had always
disliked holidays, and couldn't face the thought of one on my
own, especially in the depressed state I was in. Perhaps I could go
and make myself useful somewhere, offer my services to a
charitable organisation, sink my own troubles in the contemplation of someone else's. But I had never been a very useful sort
of person; apart from a flair for cooking, my domestic talents
were almost non-existent. Still, I *could* cook, so I had something
to offer. But to whom?

I don't really know why or how, but somehow that same
evening I found myself alone in a church. Maybe I'd gone there
to give the Almighty a last chance. Or maybe I'd just gone there
for a good howl in private. Anyway, there was no-one else in
the church, and it was a fine echo-ey building. As even when I'm

quite alone I tend to be self-conscious, I didn't howl, but muttered a defiant if muddled: 'Damn you, you don't exist, but I hate you.' Then I burst into tears, and threw decorum to the winds. 'All right,' I heard myself shouting, 'if you do exist, show me a way out. For a start, what the hell am I to do next?' After this unbridled exhibition, I was startled by the noise I was making, and ran out of the church at top speed.

Frank was in an armchair reading when I got back to the house, still tear-stained. My mother and Betty had the children in another room, where they were watching television. We had, as we always did, brought with us enough books to withstand a siege, some of them selected from the local library by Frank. Idly I picked up one of these and looked at the title: *The Face of Victory* by Group Captain Leonard Cheshire VC. I could see that it was autobiographical, and I put it down again with a grimace. Cheshire, the bomber pilot VC, had had a lot of publicity during and after the Second World War, and I was always suspicious of popular heroes. Not content with what others had written about him, I thought scornfully, he was now writing about himself. What an egoist the man must be. Frank saw the look on my face and more or less read my thoughts. 'Don't just put it down,' he urged. 'I think it would interest you. At least, give it a try.'

I had picked the book up again, and was rifling through the pages as he was speaking. As we went on talking, I stood with my thumb on one page somewhere near the end. When I put the book down it came open at that page. I stared at it, and saw that it was full of addresses, of Cheshire Homes For The Sick, where voluntary help was required. Right at the bottom, one address stuck out; a Home run not by Leonard Cheshire but by his wife, Sue Ryder. Home For Concentration Camp Survivors, Cavendish, Suffolk, I read. As I stood looking down at it, I realised that one part of my prayer in the church had been answered. I had demanded to know what I was to do next, and now I knew. I was going to Suffolk.

CHAPTER 4

Cavendish

IT WAS NOT just an off-the-cuff decision to step into the unknown.
As soon as I saw that address, I knew I had to go there; the way
had already been prepared — when I was in Louvain.

The address took me back with a jolt to the Clinique St Raphaël,
where I had spent so many interminable evenings after Paul had
been put to bed. I couldn't go out and leave him, so I had taken
to pacing the corridor outside our room, up and down aimlessly
for hours on end, past the various wards and single rooms.

One night I saw a woman wheeled on a trolley into one of the
emergency rooms, and was forcibly struck by her gaunt appearance and her sunken staring eyes. They were the eyes of a woman
haunted by some appalling and unforgettable suffering. The next
night I heard a woman scream, and knew who it must be. It
was an unearthly screeching sound, unlike anything I had ever
heard, a sort of banshee wail; and it filled me with an unbelievable
dread.

The screaming continued for an eternity of ten minutes or so,
then stopped as suddenly and as eerily as it had started, leaving
behind a silence that was full of nameless horrors. A man who
was pacing in the other direction must have seen the fear in my
eyes, and he came to join me. 'She was in Ravensbrück,' he said

quietly, with the air of one who has explained everything.
'Ravensbrück?' I asked blankly, as much in the dark as ever. The
man looked taken aback by my obvious ignorance, and proceeded
to tell me more. Ravensbrück, he explained, was the Nazi concentration camp north of Berlin, where women and children were
sent. Many of these had been subjected to medical experimenta-
tion, and many thousands had died there. (The official figure was
in fact 92,000.) This woman had been one of the guinea-pigs on
whom experiments had been carried out. She was a sorry part of
the human wreckage which had survived such camps, as much
dead as alive. The hospital was as much her home as any other
place, since she spent more time there than anywhere else.

His words sent ice-cold shivers coursing along my spine. I would
have walked away if I could, but I didn't dare. Mentally I re-
sisted him. Why did the man have to tell me such things? Couldn't
he sense that I didn't want to hear them? The war had been over
for fifteen years, its effects had been neatly tidied away. When it
had come to an end, I was still a child, and the stories coming out
of Belsen and other places of that kind had scarcely troubled me,
so great was my relief that the war was over at last. I didn't want
to listen to atrocity stories now. Hadn't I enough troubles of my
own?

But my companion, a man of about forty-five from Arlon,
had no intention of letting me off. For four years he too had
suffered in a concentration camp, Neuengamme, where only the
strongest had survived. In spite of myself, I had to listen horror-
struck to his nightmare memories: of the barely-alive prisoners
piling the dead each morning into trucks and throwing the corpses
into a specially-prepared ditch; of the six ounces of bread and two
frost-bitten potatoes on which the prisoners were forced to per-
form slave labour. Sometimes, my friend recalled, the SS cook
would fling a crust into their midst, for the sadistic pleasure of
seeing starving men scratch and claw at each other in the scramble
to stay alive. Rather than starve, they had eaten filth, keeping
themselves alive on their own excrement. My friend had come
through, but at a price. In the fifteen years which had elapsed
since the Liberation, he had continued to suffer from severe

intestinal disorders which forced him to spend one month out of every four in this hospital.

When he eventually let me go, I went back to my room and wrote in my diary, 'I shall not go out there again to-morrow. If these things happened I prefer not to know about them.' I was as good as my own cowardly word; I did not see the man from Arlon again; but I found that he was not so easy to forget. What he had told me could not be untold, and against my will it had had its effect. Every word he had spoken came unbidden to mind as I stood gazing at that address in Suffolk. With an uncanny feeling that the course of my life was being directed by powerful forces, I sat down and wrote to whoever was in charge at the Home for Concentration Camp survivors in Suffolk, offering my services for a week as bed-maker, and mentioning that I could cook. In the circumstances, it was no surprise at all when the reply came by return: Come as soon as you can, we need you urgently.

Wearing my best suit and carrying a large suitcase bulging with clothes, I passed the village duck-pond, turned into the drive of the Sue Ryder Home, and caught my first glimpse of the idyllic, pink-washed sixteenth-century house which sheltered physically handicapped patients, others who had been mentally ill, and a handful of survivors of Nazi tyranny. It was to become my own spiritual home over the next four years. The September sun was shining, and I was filled with a vague euphoria not entirely free of self-congratulation. I had come to indulge in a bout of do-gooding, and was all dressed-up to play the role of lady bountiful.

Without warning, a female figure erupted out of a mullioned window on the ground floor of the house, and hurled itself at me. 'Thank God you've come,' said the girl fervently, casting a baffled glance at my enormous suitcase, before rushing on at the same breathless speed: 'You must be the new slave. Look, the bathroom in the extension is flooded, and the water's seeped into Edward's room, and the whole place is in a terrible mess. Would you mind frightfully going over there and seeing what you can do? Good. I'll go and get a bucket and mop.' And with that she was off, leaving me feeling as bewildered as Alice accosted by the White Rabbit. I looked down at my good suit, and suddenly saw how ridiculous I must look, standing there kitted out for the London Hilton rather than for flooding bathrooms in deepest Suffolk. The girl was now back with mop and bucket. Resignedly I dumped the suitcase on the gravel, and went off in the direction in which she had pointed, mop-handle tucked under Windsmoor jacket sleeve. 'By the way,' the girl shouted after me, 'I believe you can cook. Well, when you've finished cleaning up over there, do you think you could manage supper for seventy? We've got a whole group of survivors over from Poland on the Foundation's Holiday Scheme, as well as the Bods who are always here.'

That was my introduction to Cavendish (not untypical, as I later discovered). I was sorely tempted to turn right round and head for home. Instead I meekly went off to tackle the flood.

Two days, several hundredweight of peeled potatoes and many gallons of soup later, I felt I had been there all my life.

Cavendish is an unlikely backdrop to the lives of the people who have found refuge there. It is a peaceful, sleepy village which minds its own business and does not take all that kindly to foreigners. Sue Ryder's mother had lived in the converted farm-house for several years and was much loved in the village, but when Sue moved in with her patients, Mrs Ryder, amid general mourning, went to live in the near-by village of Clare.

Sue Ryder, a tiny bird-like woman who looks vulnerable but is about as fragile as granite, was an attractive girl in her late teens when the Second World War broke out. She joined the exclusive FANYs (First Aid Nursing Yeomanry) and through them was seconded to Special Operations Executive (SOE), the highly secret organisation responsible for training agents in the difficult techniques of armed resistance and sabotage. During parachute training Sue unfortunately injured her back, and, unable as a result to be dropped behind enemy lines, she had to be content with a less active role. For the most part she worked with young Poles of both sexes who had volunteered to return to their stricken country and fight the invader from within. These young men and women knew very well that they were volunteering for almost certain torture and death, but nothing could deter them. To the young Sue they were giants; and they taught her a lesson that she would never forget: that the individual human being can do the apparently impossible, if only he cares enough.

Long before the war was over, Sue had come to realise that its aftermath would be terrible — for the whole of Europe, and in particular for those countries of Central Europe which had been occupied. As early as 1942 she had made up her mind to do relief work when the fighting stopped. 'I couldn't see, with devastation on that scale,' she says, 'how it could ever be cleared up.' She was quite prepared to give the rest of her life to caring not only for those who survived the holocaust but for the sick and disabled of all age groups in those countries where the need was greatest. Her work, she determined, would provide a 'Living Memorial' to those who had died, many of them anonymously, in two World Wars.

In the years that followed the peace she worked in different parts of Europe with various international relief organisations — until their mandate ran out. And when it did, she stayed on. 'How could I go?' she asks. Some of those who still needed her help then were adults and children in Germany who could not return to their own countries because those countries had been annexed by the Soviet Union; and there were others elsewhere who, although not exiled from their homes, were desperately trying to clear away rubble and rebuild their shattered cities and towns, battling against heavy odds to reconstruct the ruins of their lives. Then there were the non-German prisoners adrift in Germany: these were young men who had been deported to Germany at an early age and who had known only violence, brutality and the ethic of the jungle. When the war was over and they were released from the concentration and labour camps in which they had been held, they emerged to face a hostile world. Unemployed (they had no work permits) and hungry, they took the law into their own hands and lived off their wits until they were caught.

Sue began a long and lonely struggle on their behalf, battling against the German authorities for residence permits, permissions to emigrate, for jobs, homes, compensation, hospitalisation and remission of prison sentences. Initially she had 1,200 prisoners in her care — 'Boys', she called them. She would visit them in prison, taking with her the essentials — drawing-paper and text books — which were denied them by the prison authorities. As a senior colleague of hers once told me, 'those boys weren't allowed any occupational activities at all, but that cut no ice with Sue. She took things in and out of the prisons the whole time!' The fact was that Sue wanted to help the prisoners become people again; and if red tape got in the way, she would cut it.

Sue had lived in the displaced persons' camps and had made their despair her own. She knew only too well that in the face of such bottomless misery, official charity was simply not enough, that what the stranded men and women in the camps needed above all was an acknowledgment that they were still human, and accepted as such by other human beings. Their lost self-respect could not be restored by official hand-outs, it was personal service that was needed. Having decided that that alone was what counted, the young Sue Ryder determined that, whatever the cost to herself, she would give that service. (And that the cost was high no one can doubt — there are all too many signs on her face.) And so, at the time when the various international relief organisations were packing up to return home, Sue began a punishing routine: visiting camps, hospitals, prisons in an area extending from the Danish border to Austria, she lived on apples and flasks of coffee, travelling over a thousand miles a week in a small, anonymously donated, Austin car which she nicknamed 'Alice'.

'She was absolutely right', comments Joyce Pearce who, like Sue, was working in Germany in those days. 'Everyone else seemed to think of the homeless as a mass problem to be dealt with by mass solutions. But Sue's personal approach was the only real way in which they could be helped.'

She called them 'Bods' — a name which falls strangely, even harshly, on our ears today, but which was meant as a mark of deepest respect. For it was as 'Bods' that the young wartime resistance agents had been affectionately known by those who had worked with them, and for Sue the name was tinged with heroism. Her 'Bods', homeless and disabled flotsam of the war, adrift in the country which had caused their troubles in the first place, needed now to be found a permanent home. Every time she returned to England, Sue searched for suitable places, but she could find nothing that she could afford. Then one day her mother, always a staunch ally, made the suggestion which had already half-occurred to her daughter: why not bring some of them to Cavendish?

They came. Marie, for example, who had lost both her arms when thrown from a moving train by her SS guards, yet who polished furniture with her feet and did fine embroidery with the needle held in her teeth; white-haired Pani Jozefa, in her early fifties yet looking like an old woman of eighty — in Auschwitz for more than three years, and sent out from there on a death march which few were meant to or did survive; Edward, a Polish lawyer of distinction, who had languished for six months in the infamous Pawiak prison in Warsaw, before being despatched to five years in Dachau and Flossenburg; Mr Bor who put his whole heart into making chicken-meal for the Cavendish hens, as he tried to blot out his past. Mr Bor had been imprisoned in the Warsaw Ghetto, from which he and a handful of others had managed to escape through a sewer. Joining the official underground, he became a vital link in an escape chain which smuggled Jewish children out of the Ghetto. But the Gestapo caught him, and sent him to Auschwitz.*

* See pp. 49 – 50.

Then there was Kasi, still a young man in his thirties, who had, in his teens, been beaten up by SS guards using rifle butts, so that he was now no more than an animated vegetable, mute and semi-paralysed. I remember vividly trying to feed him one night, putting a spoonful of fish into his mouth, while salty tears ran down my face into the spoon. All the ills of the world seemed to be concentrated here in Cavendish, massively ignored by the world outside. There were residents who suffered from epilepsy-type attacks, the result of earlier skull injuries; others with dissemin-ated sclerosis or psychiatric disorders: schizophrenia, paranoia or delusions great and small. These men and women had reached this quiet Suffolk back-water by way of some of the greatest hells ever devised on earth, Belsen, Buchenwald, Majdanek, Ravensbrück and Auschwitz, and, on the way, everything that had given their lives value and meaning had been stripped from them. There were others, too, who had come here after months and years in imper-sonal long-stay hospitals, where they had been 'blocking' the beds needed for short-term 'acute' patients; and some who, foreign nationals, had lived and worked in England since the war, before disablement or mental breakdown struck.

As long as I live, I shall never be able to forget that first visit to Cavendish, because it changed my whole life. It was all so unexpected and disturbing. In theory I knew that I was coming to a home for the disabled. In practice I had little idea of what that meant. I was mentally unprepared to discover, in this peaceful part of rural England, an island of pain, an enduring reminder of man's extreme brutality towards his fellow-man. And an even more forceful reminder of the outside world's capacity for for-getting what it does not want to remember — except in terms of harmless statistics. Cavendish was a place where statistics had become persons.

At first, as I peeled potatoes by the bucketful, sliced innumerable cabbages for the *bigos* beloved of Poles, and immersed myself elbow-deep in beetroots for the inevitable *barszcz* ('Are your arms always that colour?' asked Leonard Cheshire with interest, catching me at it in the kitchen), I was aware only of the terrible suffering which these people had endured, and of the limbo in in which they now only half-existed. The shock of the discovery was tremendous. But after a few days, I began to notice something else: I was actually singing as I peeled those eternal spuds. The amazing truth took some time to sink in: Cavendish, against all the odds, was a happy place. Its serenity was catching. It was good to be there.

Slowly I came to know the 'Bods'. I would watch them in the morning, at the start of another, for them painful, day. Mr Bor would be stirring up messes for his chicken-pails. Then along came Mr Crab, shuffling with difficulty on two sticks towards the dining-room for breakfast. 'Good morning, Sister,' he shouted cheerfully to Margaret, the resident nurse. 'A beautiful morning, Mr Crab,' she replied, using the nickname by which he was always known. 'Fanta-a-a-stic morning, ma-a-arvellous sunshine,' echoed 'Bubi', a Czech originally from Prague who was crippled with arthritis, but was noted for his sunny disposition. ('Bubi' played the piano like an angel, despite his crippled hands, and on these occasions he was accompanied by his great friend Ben, a Hungarian, on the trombone. Bubi's room looked out over the tree-fringed pond and what he called God's garden. 'There is my chapel, it is all that I need,' he would say, pointing to the garden. When he was well enough he would spend hours looking out at it, but when he was sad, or the pain was too acute, he turned his back on it, as though he could not bear to look on beauty. Bubi loved life in all its manifestations. 'A party,' he cried delightedly, when I turned up to see him at Cavendish shortly before he died, 'we must have a party to celebrate. Go quickly to the shop, Mary, and get some ham.' Laboriously he counted out the money for me. When I came back, he had magicked a couple of plates onto the bed. I could see that he was in pain, but nothing could have damped his spirits that afternoon, as he laughed and sang, and we ate our ham with dry biscuits, and toasted each other with Nescafé. It is my last memory of him, and one that I shall always treasure.)

Little Mr Szkoda followed Bubi into the dining-room, coming in whistling from the garden where he had been digging potatoes. 'Little man with a hoe' is how I remember him. And Kasi brought up the rear of the procession, shambling along awkwardly like an injured bear, winking surreptitiously at one of the pretty 'slaves' who was serving breakfast.

The 'slaves', as the helpers called themselves, were pretty remarkable too. They were all girls who were capable of holding down good jobs with an excellent salary. Yet they were working full-time (round the clock, in shifts, not nine-to-five) at Cavendish for nothing, or for a derisory two pounds a week pocket-money. They were there because they could not conceive of being anywhere else, because they believed in the value of what they were doing. There was something very special about Cavendish, its people and its atmosphere, which called forth this kind of special devotion.

As I talked to the 'Bods', I began to understand that what I had stumbled on at Cavendish was a kind of miracle. These people had, as it were, walked into the valley of death, and out the other side, with their courage and their sense of humour intact. They were rich human beings, with no bitterness left in them. For years they had walked with starvation, torture, cold, loneliness and agonising loss. Yet they seemed to be beyond hatred. To me it was bewildering.

In fact I was being shaken up and turned inside out. Suddenly it seemed as though my whole life had been leading up to this one time and this one place, to which I had been sent (I was entirely sure of it) in order to come to terms with the problem of suffering in my own life. Somewhere here there was a key, and I must set myself to find it. I had gone to Cavendish to get away from my own troubles, to sort myself out by offering help to someone else, doubtless in the pious hope that such undeniable signs of virtue would bring their own reward. But all I had been doing was looking for a place to hide. What had I imagined I could possibly give these people, when there was nothing in me to give? Hadn't I been systematically surrounding myself with impregnable defences, protecting myself from hurt? I hadn't overcome self-pity, I'd merely been keeping it at bay; it was lying low just outside my defences, biding its time, gathering strength for the next, more vicious attack.

The survivors showed me another possibility: that one could live with pain precisely by not fighting it; by not denying its existence, by taking it into oneself, seeing it for what it was, using it, going beyond it. Precisely how I could not yet see; but I knew it could be done. I had tangible proof. If men could laugh after Auschwitz, then surely there was hope. My cure had not yet got under weigh, but by great good fortune I had found both the right doctor and the only possible medicine.

What happened to Mr Bor a few years later is worth the telling, if only to show that fairy-tales still happen. Stefan Bor, left an orphan at a very early age, had been brought up in the family of a friend, and in his teens had fallen in love with Zofia, the daughter of the house. Before they could marry, they were overtaken by the war and the Occupation; both of them joined the Resistance; both were arrested. They were sent to different camps and they never saw each other again.

Or at least they hadn't, when I first went to Cavendish. Mr Bor looked after his ducks and hens, and from time to time he spoke about Zofia, who was, he said, his sister. One day, he added, when he had acquired British nationality, he would go to Poland and look for her. An old man's dream, we thought.

But that is exactly what he did. When he was nearly seventy, Stefan Bor became Stephen Burton, and went to Poland in search of his lost love. Against all the odds he found her; and against

4

longer odds still, she had waited for him, sure that he would come.

When he returned to Cavendish, he revealed to an astonished Sue Ryder that Zofia was not his sister but was now his fiancée, and that she was coming to England to marry him. Zofia too was nearly seventy when she left home to make the historic journey. Landing alone at Harwich, she walked towards her waiting husband-to-be, scattering handfuls of the Polish soil she had brought with her for the purpose, enacting a typically Polish bit of symbolism. 'Your country, she is now my country,' she announced with pride.

On 31st October 1967, almost thirty years late, Zofia and Stephen Burton were married in the timbered chapel of Clare Priory in Suffolk, a long way from Auschwitz. No couple ever approached the altar with greater faith in their future together; they had already proved their total steadfastness.

They were together for seven years — that is, until Stefan/Stephen died in 1974. His widow is still living at the Sue Ryder Home in Cavendish.

CHAPTER 5

Paul Goes to Poland

THE JOURNEY HOME from Cavendish after that first visit passed as though in a dream. I was high — on memories. The links I had forged in that one short week, the friendships I had made, would be impossible to break. Among others, I had got to know Leonard Cheshire, who was at home recuperating from a serious illness; and my earlier suspicion that he was nothing more than a glamorous play-boy had given way to an enduring affection and admiration.

But although I had seen much less of his wife, Sue Ryder, during that week, she was the one for whom I wanted to work. I wanted to tell the world about her and what she was doing for that handful of people from a forgotten world. Frank came to meet me at the station, and as we drove home I began to try and explain. But I stopped in mid-stream because of the hopelessness of conveying the enormity of what I felt. 'So you've found your life's work,' he commented with a smile. I interrupted him sharply, near to tears, 'Please don't laugh. It's very important.' 'Who's laughing?' he asked. 'I can see something has happened to you. Tell me about it, and I'll try to help.' He really meant it, and his words were a tremendous relief.

From then on, I became a one-track bore, and it is amazing

that friends did not desert me in droves. All conversations led to Sue Ryder and the people at Cavendish. It became a matter of extreme urgency to let everyone know about them. An initial trickle of invitations to speak became a flood, and soon I found myself talking to most of the local organisations in Cheshire and Lancashire — Rotary Clubs, Inner Wheels, Townswomen's Guilds, Ladies' Circles, Round Tables, Women's Institutes. Fortunately I discovered a hitherto unsuspected talent for public speaking, and for getting across to people — it must have been because I cared about the subject so deeply. But, however much I cared, I could have got nowhere without the enthusiastic support and continuing commitment of the people to whom I was speaking. Slowly a network of support groups came into being, first in the Manchester area and then beyond, all of them intent on raising funds for Sue Ryder, not only for the Home at Cavendish, but for the sister-Home at Hickleton Hall near Doncaster, which had the advantage of being almost on the doorstep, and for Sue's work in Poland and Yugoslavia as well. Girls from the school where I taught (and from others where I gave talks) went in groups to help out at Cavendish or Hickleton in the holidays, and a few of them became as addicted as I was, going back again and again. One girl decided to train to be a nurse, and eventually returned to Hickleton as a nursing sister.

At first the support-groups held the usual coffee mornings, bazaars and lunches, until in 1963 we opened our first second-hand shop. To-day charity shops dot the High Streets of Britain like measles, but at that time they were relatively unknown. Sue Ryder had always been keen on the idea, and on the day that she was offered rent-free premises in Manchester she rang me up. 'Do take it, Mary,' she urged. 'We could make anything from £7–£10 a week, and we can't afford to turn away that kind of money.' Our marvellous Manchester supporters, led by Bessie Galpin and Eileen Ruhemann, leaped at the chance, organised themselves into relays, and within a short while had opened a shop in Rusholme (Manchester). This was almost immediately followed by three more in the Manchester area and eventually by dozens more throughout the country. We sold out everything we had on the first afternoon, but it didn't seem to matter. Miraculously we had found an ever-lasting fountain. Goods to sell, and volunteers eager and willing to help kept coming, and in that first week we made not £7 but nearly £100 — mainly on junk. That was fifteen years ago. Since then the Rusholme shop and others like and unlike it — in wealthy areas as well as poor — selling new articles as well as second-hand — have become the mainstay of the Sue Ryder Foundation. They are very different from each other in scope and merchandise but they have one thing in common. All of them make money for the relief of suffering.

But the shops were not my forte. Leaving them to others more capable, and with more stamina, I went on with the talks. Nervous as a kitten beforehand, I felt sick to the pit of my stomach, at least until I began to speak. Whether it was an audience of hundreds in Manchester's Free Trade Hall or a huddle of two on a foggy night in somebody's shed, I was equally nervous. But the warmth of response made up for the agony of nerves.

Some knew what I had come for, others did not, and in the beginning could not care less. 'It is my privilege to introduce Mrs Craig, a . . . er . . . star of stage, screen and radio,' announced one headmistress, realising too late that she hadn't a clue who I was (or was not). The stolid ranks of pupils looked surprised, to say the least. But I was not always up-graded like that. One Chairwoman gestured at me with her hand: 'We have with us to-night Miss -er, Mrs -er er-, who is going to tell us about — er, well, she'll tell you all about it herself, and I'm sure you'll all enjoy it.' The audience applauded this masterly introduction, though some of them were halfway through a row of knitting, and some were to all appearances asleep. One of them came to talk to me afterwards. 'We were ever so surprised,' she confessed. 'We thought you were going to talk about family planning. We must have got the weeks mixed up.' Doubtless the ladies were disappointed on that occasion; but perhaps not so much as the group to whom I was announced as 'the well-known superinten-dent of concentration camps'.

For six years I kept up the pace, and maintained the split personality; one week being the special 'weren't-we-lucky-to-get-hold-of-her' guest-speaker at an annual rally or exclusive luncheon club, and the next being mistaken for last week's Flower Arrangement, or being rung by a harassed Secretary at the eleventh hour because 'Mrs Jones was going to show us her colour slides of Bermuda, but she's got flu, and would you come instead?' On one such occasion a woman accosted me on the way out. 'I was looking forward to Mrs Jones's colour-slides,' she said accusingly. 'If I'd realised she wasn't going to be here, I shouldn't have come.' She was very indignant.

All this time, things were coming together for me. The more I talked to people about the survivors, and came to identify with them, understanding more and more about their lives, the more I found that I was helping myself to understand my own situation. The lesson I was learning was that though pain has the capacity to destroy it may also be creative. Just how much I was to owe to the survivors, as yet I fortunately did not know. For the time was not far off when I would identify with them even more closely.

For a while, perhaps a year, Paul went daily to a Junior Training Centre in Altrincham. He loved it, and loved being surrounded by other children, but the staff found it very hard to cope with his disastrous incontinence. He was one person's job, and, in a school which at that time was as short of staff as it was of facilities, he was more than they could handle. Nowadays schools for the mentally handicapped are better equipped to deal with children like Paul (there are special-care units for the more difficult and more disabled children), but fifteen years ago things were different. On one or two occasions, when visitors were expected at the Centre, the Superintendent asked us to keep Paul at home. It was the thin end of the wedge, as we were well aware. From there it was a short step to asking us to keep him at home altogether. The Superintendent saw this as a perfectly reasonable request, and while the Training Centres were still under the aegis of the Ministry of Health rather than of Education, she was quite within her rights. When, a few years later, they passed into the control of the Ministry of Education, children like Paul were given security of tenure. Paul was unlucky. His 'schooldays' were brief, but they had been happy.

Paul had no speech, no means of communication, no powers of retention, no ability to concentrate. The hardest thing of all was that he didn't know us, and couldn't become a member of the family in any really positive sense. He stayed marooned in the playroom downstairs, a lonely little figure, face permanently squashed against the window-pane, uttering strange, incomprehensible sounds.

Several times he almost died. During a tonsillectomy he began to haemorrhage badly, but in spite of a heavy loss of blood, he pulled through. The bronchitis that he had suffered from since babyhood never relinquished its hold, and twice he was rushed off to hospital black in the face. One night he had fifteen bronchial convulsions. I was advised to spend the night at the hospital, and at about midnight the doctor came in to see me. 'It looks like the end,' he said, 'you'd better be prepared.' 'I always am,' I answered. But by daybreak Paul had thumbed his nose at death once again and lay sleeping peacefully.

In spite of our disappointment over the earlier treatment, we were still prepared to try anything or go anywhere that offered any hope. I don't think it was a question of believing that anything could be done, so much as the feeling that making some sort of move was preferable to standing still.

It was Sue Ryder who precipitated the next move. We had become friends, and she had often spoken of a Polish friend of hers, a neuropsychiatrist, who had achieved some astounding successes in the treatment of mentally-handicapped children. 'If only Dr W. could see Paul,' she kept saying, 'I know he would try to help him. He's the one man in the world who could.' One evening she telephoned. Dr W. was in England for a Conference on mental health, and he had come to see her. Delighted as she was, she had promptly put him on a train for Manchester, and he was at that moment on his way to us. I thanked her for the kind thought, but couldn't think how he could help. But Sue does nothing by halves, and she had another bolt to shoot. 'One more thing, Mary,' she said, as if it were an afterthought. 'If Dr W. suggests Paul going to him in Poland, do let him go.' Then she rang off in a rush, before I could get my breath back.

The idea was preposterous, unthinkable, and I was quite sure that Sue had taken leave of her senses. Taking Paul to Louvain was one thing. Abandoning him in Central Europe was something else. Impossible. Or that was the way it seemed before we met Dr W. He was different from all the others, even the Belgians. He didn't treat Paul as just another interesting case, but as a person; and he didn't itemise the clinical symptoms as though Paul were an inanimate object, but singled out a few limited areas where there might be some hope. He not only examined Paul minutely, but he won his trust and confidence, and, in so far as it was possible, his affection too. He stayed with us for two days, after which he was quite clear in his mind that he would like to take the matter further. With Sue's last words still ringing in my ears (and they no longer sounded quite so fantastic) I was not altogether surprised when he asked us if Paul could go to him in Poland for a year or so. There was a hope, a very slender one, but a hope just the same, that he could bring about an improvement in Paul's condition, and he was very anxious to try.

What decided us in the end to let Paul go was not so much the prospect of some great improvement as the fact of his present isolation. Now that he was excluded from the Training Centre and was at home all the time, he no longer had the company of other children. He was eight years old and had loved being with the others. It was tragic now to see his lonely face pressed all daylong against the playroom window. If he went to Dr W.'s children's sanatorium, he would have all the company he needed.

Sue was delighted and set about making the arrangements. Dr W. had come to us in November, and Sue wrote from Poland in the following February to say that everything was fixed up. It was better than we could have hoped for. The Polish Ministry of Health had turned down our offer of maintenance payment and were prepared, in consideration of my own (extremely limited) services to the work of the Sue Ryder Trust in Poland, to take Paul for two years free of charge. We could hardly believe in our good fortune.

In September of the same year, Paul and I set off for Warsaw.

Once again I was hopeful, but I was keeping in mind the cautionary letter Leonard Cheshire had sent me just before I left: 'Something inside me makes me want to say to you, don't count on it too much,' he wrote. 'Dr W. is an outstanding man, and we all pray that he really can do what he hopes to do for Paul. But please, Mary, don't raise your hopes too high.'

The sanatorium, which housed four hundred children, was about an hour and a half's drive outside of Warsaw, on the road to Lublin. The village which housed it was poor, and the place itself had been an old barracks, ugly and ramshackle from the outside. Inside the grounds, however, newer, handsomer buildings were springing up, and in one of the annexes Paul was to be lodged, sharing a room with Richard, a boy of about the same age from Chicago.

One place was the same as another to Paul, and he was quite happy to go off with a woman doctor as soon as we arrived. When later I was taken on a guided tour of the hospital and came across him, he showed no sign of recognition. He was wandering round a playground with a young nurse, and when I approached he looked straight through me. The Chicago boy, Richard, was there too, and he, not Paul, gave me a kiss. One thing I could be quite sure of, I was not going to be missed.

I left there a week later. My last sight of Paul was sitting at a table with some little spastic children, being helped to ring sausage and dill pickles. English food, Polish food, it was all one to him, so long as it was food. There was an expression of pure bliss on his face. I was crying as I bent over to kiss him, but his only response was one of his deep chortles.

As I left the hospital with Dr W., a number of children seemed to appear from nowhere to join us, drawn by his undeniably magnetic presence. I thought of him then, as often later, as a kind of Hans Andersen figure, irresistible to children of any age. I knew I could not be leaving Paul in better hands, but that didn't prevent me feeling tearful. But I had only my own feelings to worry about, not Paul's. It was one occasion when I could be thankful that Paul didn't know one place, or one person, from another.

In many ways, I felt relief as I boarded the plane at Okecie

Airport outside Warsaw: a new baby was expected in January. With Paul in safe keeping for a year or two, I could look forward to enjoying the baby without having my hands impossibly full, and my attention inevitably elsewhere.

CHAPTER 6

Nicholas

SUE RYDER WAS going to be godmother. I had told her about the
baby as soon as I knew that I was pregnant. On the phone I was
gloomy. 'What if the baby shouldn't be alright?' I speculated. She
brushed away such unprofitable fears. 'Of course it'll be alright,'
she said. 'You really mustn't start getting morbid.'

On the night of January 18th 1965 I went into the nursing-
home in Bowdon, near where we lived. The matron was the
friend of a friend of mine, and she had taken a special interest in
me. Nothing, she said, must be allowed to go wrong, and she
would make a point of attending to me herself.

It was the usual sort of labour, the familiar mixture of intolerable and merely awful; there were no special problems. I don't
remember the actual moment of birth, but I have a painfully clear
memory of hearing two nurses talking in the labour ward afterwards, while I was still no more than semi-conscious. 'Oh no, not
another boy,' said one, 'what a disappointment for her.' I recall
the slight stab of disappointment, because both of us had badly
wanted a girl. Then the other one replied: 'Another boy! Dear
God, if that were all she had to worry about!' That was all. Half-
under though I was, the meaning of the words reached me, and
I was touched with nightmare dread.

When I came to, I was in a small, two-bedded ward with another young mother. 'Hello, are you alright?' she asked, as I opened my eyes. I looked at her. 'I'm not sure,' I said, 'I think there's something wrong with the baby.' 'Oh no,' she said reassuringly, 'you must have had a bad dream.' Well, maybe she was right, I thought. But just then a young nurse came into the room. She scurried around doing whatever it was she'd come in to do, and whisked out again like a frightened rabbit who'd glimpsed a stoat. I had opened my mouth to ask her a question, but she avoided meeting my eye. That was the moment when I knew, beyond any possible doubting, that what I had dreaded most had actually happened.

It seemed like an eternity later when my doctor, Joe, came in. He was half-Italian and very emotional. At this moment he was tense and unhappy, obviously nerving himself for an ordeal. He sat down by the bed.

'I don't know how to tell you, Mary,' he began.

'I think I already know,' I told him.

'What do you mean? How can you know? I don't know what you're talking about.'

'There's something wrong with the baby, that's all I know. You'd better tell me and get it over with.'

Joe looked at me, opened his mouth to say something, then put his head in his hands and cried silently. Afterwards he recovered himself sufficiently to tell me that the child was a mongol. Not a very bad case, a hairline case, I think he said. But a mongol nonetheless. Not like Paul. There seemed to be absolutely no connection between the two cases. The odds against this sort of thing happening were several hundred thousand to one. Astronomical odds which had defied probability and caught us. If nothing else, we had made medical history.

When Joe had gone, I tried to shut out all thought, because all thoughts led back to the same intolerable one: we now had two mentally handicapped sons, not one. I was screaming inside.

When Frank came to see me that afternoon, he couldn't trust himself to speak, any more than I could. He held my hand, while we both stayed silent, frightened by the enormity of the blow and the collapse of our hopes. Even now, years later, we have never told each other what we felt when we first heard the news. There are feelings too deep for sharing.

The prospect of the long night hours ahead filled me with dread. I didn't see how I could get through them without being destroyed by the fear, anger, panic and shame that were raging inside me. Everything was falling to pieces. The tender shoot of understanding, the fragile hold I had got on the meaning of suffering were swallowed up in the whirlpool in which I was now drowning. Prayer? Not likely. I'd finished with that. I'd tried it, and look where it had got me.

And so the night came on, and I slipped further and further into the abyss. Past fears mingled with future terrors, and I thought I was losing my reason. As the fears grew more monstrous, my own descent to darkness accelerated. I was spinning in an endlessly twisting spiral.

It was when I had given up hope of ever reaching the bottom, that some words I had once read flashed into my mind with brilliant clarity: 'Our tragedy is not that we suffer, but that we waste suffering. We waste the opportunity of growing into compassion.' The words leaped out at me, acting like a brake on my despair, dramatically halting my slide into madness.

What happened at that moment was the only mystical experience I have ever known, and there are no words to describe its intensity. It seemed to me that suddenly I was held firm, safe from further falling, and a voice inside me was saying: 'there is a way through this, but you must find it outside of yourself. Remember I am here, in the darkness. You are never alone.'

The words from the prayer-book were still there, weaving themselves into my consciousness. Somehow mixed up with them I could see a group of people – the 'Bods', those survivors of disaster far worse than this, who had pointed a way through for me once before. I was linked to them by a fine thread, and I understood that now I had become one of them. Others joined them, and then others, and though they drifted in a mist of anonymity I knew that they were all linked together by common suffering. And, on the horizon, a Cross, radiating light over the entire assembly. In accepting the symbolism, that the love which triumphed from the Cross could alone save men from themselves, I would find the promise of peace.

Next morning, the flowers began to arrive, bringing with them an almost tangible awareness of supportive love and grief. The first to arrive were from colleagues at the Loreto Convent where I had been a part-time teacher, and the accompanying message was sad and uncomprehending. Without further thought, I reached for paper and pen, and wrote to console them, trying to put what had happened into perspective for them. Suddenly I realised that my 'vision' had borne fruit. In some mysterious way, it was my friends who needed comforting more than I, and I wanted to reach out to them and help them to understand.

Congratulations cards were conspicuous by their absence, but in their place came letters. No-one in their right mind could say that they were happy for us, but almost everyone I had ever known, even only slightly, felt impelled to write, to express deep feelings, or even to apologise for the fact that they did not know how to. One letter which moved me to tears said simply: 'We just don't know what to say, except that you have our love and prayers.' The letters formed a solid wall of affection – some of them were blotchy with tears – which was a far more powerful support than their writers could have realised. The awareness that barriers were down, reserves dropped, differences forgotten, was profoundly healing. People who were normally inarticulate strove to pour out on paper what they had felt on hearing the news. Many said, 'Talking to you would be easier,' but they were mistaken. The letters, representing as they did, so much human feeling, so much anguished groping for words, said more than the spoken word ever could. They could be looked at over and over again, they had a strength out of all proportion to their actual stumbling content, and I still have them all. Had they offered glib religious consolation, or pious hopes of a better world to come, they would have been difficult to take. It was the sheer floundering incoherence of so many of them that made them important and precious. I felt I was being upheld by a genuine human response, and it seemed to me the most powerful force in all the world. Those letters did not take the place of prayer, they *were* prayer.

A French friend who lived nearby in Bowdon, underlined for me what I was feeling very strongly, that even this latest hammer-blow had meaning and purpose. She sent some lines of a French poem which summed it up exactly:

Et crois-tu donc distrait le Dieu qui t'a frappé?
L'homme est un apprenti, la douleur est son maître,
Et nul ne se connaît tant qu'il n'a pas souffert.

(Do you imagine that it is in a fit of absent-mindedness that God has afflicted you? We have so much to learn, and grief must be our master. It is only through suffering that we can hope to come to self-knowledge.)

Buoyed up though I was with all this affection, I couldn't help but be aware of the handful of friends who had not written, among them two who were closest to me. I fretted about their silence, and did not realise that it might reflect the intensity of their grief rather than indifference. One of them wrote later, 'I refused to let myself write to you at the time, because I didn't want to intrude upon whatever little privacy you had. I know that there are moments when one simply wants to hide away from everybody.' No, I hadn't felt like that, but I should have known that she would see things that way. That is the way she would have wanted it in similar circumstances. As for the other friend, I did not know till years later that she had rung my mother to see if the baby had arrived, and on receiving the news had fled to her room, locked herself in, and cried for two days. Months after I came out of hospital, I met her briefly. 'Why couldn't you have written?' I asked bitterly. 'Even just a line to show that you cared.' My own fretting had turned into hostility, and she lacked the courage to explain that she had made several attempts to write but had given them up. Thirteen years passed before we saw each other again, and renewed our friendship as strongly as before. She told me then that ever since that time she had always written immediately to anyone she knew to be in any kind of trouble. 'I had never realised how important it was until then,' she said. I regretted the hostility I had felt, and I had learned something I should have known: that silence does not always mean indifference.

CHAPTER 7

Breaking the Shell

THE BABY WAS called Nicholas Peter, and he was exactly a month old when I first saw him. The Matron at the nursing-home was unwilling to disturb me further for the first day or so, and I have to admit that, in spite of my resolve to accept the situation and use it for good in some way, I was in no hurry to take the first practical step — that of holding the baby in my arms and loving him. For the moment I had to face the simple fact that I was no less a coward than I had always been.

Then matters were taken out of my hands. Complications were discovered. The baby had been born without a rectum, and within half an hour of the discovery had been transferred to a large Children's Hospital in Central Manchester. There he was hurriedly baptised and an emergency operation was carried out.

When they told me, all my noble resolution evaporated into an unworthy hope that he would die. It was a fifty-fifty chance: he was very young to undergo such a serious operation. Shamelessly, I wanted those odds to lessen. I wanted a way out. At this stage, Nicholas was no more than an unfortunate happening, and now there was a distinct hope that the misfortune might be blotted out. God, how I wanted that to happen.

Nicky, of course, survived — so there was no way out. One

65

day in early February Frank and I went over to the hospital to
see him. When we were taken to his cot, a chill struck both
of us. He hardly looked like a baby at all. A pathetic little object
strapped to the cot, with tubes sticking out of every aperture. I
felt a disbelieving sense of nightmare, a horror undiluted by any
tender feelings. I can't pretend that I felt any love for that tiny child.
Pity, yes, but most of all horror, because this was my child, and
very soon now he would be coming home to me. I hoped more
than ever that he would die.

A few weeks later Nicky came home. The tubes were gone,
but he had a colostomy, an opening on the abdomen instead of
the normal rectum. In a year's time he was to return to the
hospital to have the colostomy closed up and a false rectum
provided. Meanwhile we should have to learn to adapt to the
colostomy.

He was the most pathetic waif I had ever seen; and there was
so much wrong with him. Something happened to all of us that
first evening; we all became his devoted slaves. Perhaps it was his
helplessness, I don't know. What I do know is that before that
first evening was out, we loved him, and there was no more
wishing that he would die. From then on the struggle was to
keep him alive.

We began to look for the positive elements of life with Nicky.
He was lovable and loving, and he would always need us. The
paediatrician had told us that he would make limited progress,
and that what little there was would be in spurts, so that there
would be vast acreages of time in which nothing would seem to
happen. So we set our sights low. If we didn't expect much, we
could not be disappointed. It was amazing what a difference this
readjustment of attitude made. Instead of looking for signs of progress and fretting if they did not appear, we were now delighted
by the least thing. Our hopes for Nicky stood in no danger
of being thwarted, because we had none. This second disappointment must have been a cruel blow to Frank, but he did not say
so, and he never complained. As a support he was like a rock.

The first few times I went out shopping with Nicky in the
pram, I was well aware that a few people were discreetly crossing

the road to avoid the embarrassment of meeting me. I knew enough now to realise that there was no malice or scorn in this, only fear and inadequacy: they were bereft of words to fit the occasion. Not being able to coo over the new baby, they would be transfixed by anxiety about what to say. Better to dodge the issue by avoiding a meeting. I learned to make the first move myself to avoid this kind of stalemate. Giving a cheerful greeting and a smile, were ways of ensuring that they could come to terms with their lack of savoir-faire. If I came face to face with someone who quite obviously wished she was a hundred miles away, and desperately talked about the weather, I would bring up the tabu subject myself and strip its terrors away by talking about it naturally. Slowly the neighbours relaxed, and people would come and talk to Nicky in his pram with as little embarrassment as they talked to normal babies.

When I finally stopped feeling sorry for myself, I found myself beginning to think deeply about the whole problem of grief and suffering in our lives. More and more I was convinced that, though suffering was itself negative, it could very easily destroy. On the other hand it could be used positively, for growth. It was, in fact, the only means of emotional growth, the route from winter to spring. 'Your pain,' wrote Kahlil Gibran, in 'The Prophet', 'is the breaking of the shell that encloses your understanding. Even as the stone of the fruit must break, that its heart may stand in the sun, so must you know pain.' That seemed to me to reach the heart of the matter. I knew that, in my own case, however hard I had been trying to come to terms with the tragedy I had in effect been shutting out the pain, trying to deaden my awareness of it, allowing a rock-hard shell to form and insulate me from it. The mother of a school-friend had written: 'I realise that some people have interpreted your courage as hardness, but that is often the only possible way to counter such a devastating blow.' Was it? Perhaps for a time it was. Building up the shell *was* an answer, but in the end it was a rotten answer; and until that shell could be smashed, there was no hope of personal growth.

Nicky's birth was giving me a second chance, smashing that

hard shell with hammer-blows. I was left vulnerable, and when one is vulnerable one has the humility to learn.

It was all a question now of learning to take this new pain into myself so that it could become creative. To do that, I should have to face the facts head on, hiding nothing, neither exaggerating nor playing down. To see my situation exactly as it was, to go forward from there, that was the secret.

Inevitably that could only be a beginning, but it was a good one. A calm, clear appraisal of reality is the crossing of the Rubicon in a situation of this sort. There is no going back, but the land ahead is unknown, and the roads are all uncharted. 'Here be dragons' a-plenty, but the worst enemy, that composite of self-delusion and self-pity, has been identified, and at least some of its power to destroy has gone.

CHAPTER 8

Journey to Poland

IN THE SUMMER of 1965, leaving Nicky in the capable hands of Betty and my mother, I went to Poland with Sue Ryder, to see Paul, and to see something of her work among the chronic sick in that country. It was more than a journey, it was a spiritual odyssey, and it set the seal on everything I had been thinking over the last few months.

In the many talks I had given about the work of Sue Ryder, I had often described the situation in Poland in post-war years, although I had no first-hand experience of it. Poland had suffered more than any other European country from the war and the Nazi occupation; and Warsaw suffered more devastation than any other capital city. Heavily bombarded in 1939, it experienced two further catastrophes before the war was over. The first was the total destruction by the Germans of the Warsaw Ghetto, almost every inhabitant of which had been murdered or deported to concentration camps by 1943. The second was the 1944 Rising, when the SS killed or maimed the Resistance forces with un-imaginable ferocity, and Hitler sent a personal telegram to the General in charge of the operation, ordering him to raze Warsaw to the ground. By 1945 the death toll in the city was about eight hundred thousand, and, when rebuilding began, about a quarter of a million bodies were found under the debris and in the city's sewers. An estimated 90% of Warsaw's buildings were destroyed: on the left bank of the Vistula there was scarcely one left undamaged. Destruction was systematic, apocalyptic: homes, schools, hospitals, churches, were, if not obliterated, open to the sky. Men and women returning from the death camps of Auschwitz or Lublin – and indeed from all over Europe – were forced to live in ruined shells, without gas, electricity, running water, transport, telephones, and with very little food. In an economy that was struggling to drag itself out of chaos (with no outside aid), the chronic sick stood little chance. And yet, thanks to the war, the number of chronic sick was multiplying and many of them lived in incalculable poverty and distress.

During her war-service with SOE, working mainly in the Polish section, Sue had admired the tremendous courage of the young Polish agents, and she felt a deep sorrow for the ruin which had befallen their country during the Nazi occupation. The war over, she wanted to help repair that ruin in any way she could; and on her first visit to Warsaw, after meeting with ministers, doctors, nurses and social workers, that way stood clear before her. She would provide Homes for the many categories of chronic sick, particularly for those suffering from cancer. In post-war Poland thousands were dying of cancer each year, without hope of hospitalisation, drugs to relieve the pain or even, frequently, running water.

The Sue Ryder Foundation and the Polish Ministry of Health came to an agreement. If the Foundation would provide buildings, the Poles would make themselves responsible for the maintenance and staffing of each Home. And so the first of many Sue Ryder Homes came into being, and for some years teams of tradesmen belonging to the Foundation were sent to Poland, for periods varying from six months to three years, to erect new Homes and renovate the older ones.

Sue never forgot that what she had set out to provide was personal service, the kind of which no State institution is capable. She took it on herself to visit all the Homes regularly, to chat with the occupants, get to know their personal stories, discover their hidden as well as their obvious needs. She also spread the word around that whenever she came to Poland she would be available for anybody who wanted to see her, particularly for the many people, sick in either mind or body, for whom no place could be found in a Sue Ryder Home.

All this I knew, but somehow, when I came to experience the reality it was more poignant.

We set off from Cavendish early one morning. I had arrived the previous evening to find the driveway humming with industry. At the centre of the fuss, standing solidly in the golden evening sunlight, was Elijah, the giant Austin van, latest of a line of Biblical prophets, successor to Daniel, Jeremiah and Joshua. It was obvious that loading had been going on for days; 'Bods' and 'slaves' were clambering in and out and on top of Elijah, off-loading into him what seemed like the entire contents of the Home. I watched open-mouthed (and not in the least disposed to join in), as the cargo mounted: provisions, sheets, mattresses, blankets, winter clothing, bed-jackets, second-hand fur coats, wedding dresses (dozens of them), wheel-chairs, sewing-machines, hot-water bottles with hand-knitted covers, bedpans, medical samples, jars of coffee, oranges and home-made cakes. It was an incredible sight, and I felt bemused watching the endless procession of boxes, cartons, bales and tins of every possible size, shape and description, all carefully labelled for their precise destinations. All these things were now being hauled on to the top of Elijah as his innards would accept no more.

A sudden thought struck me, and I ventured forward and took a look inside the driving-compartment. Apart from a few feet of space around the driving-wheel, I could detect no other sign of a vacuum into which I, the passenger, might squeeze. 'Where,' I asked with a sinking feeling, 'am I supposed to sit?' 'There, of course,' said Sue briefly, raising an impatient eyebrow at the silliness of the question, and indicating a stack of pillows, bed-jackets, petrol cans, thermos flasks and a kettle, waiting to be loaded onto what had once been a seat. 'You'll have to sit on those.' I could see it would be futile to pursue the matter – she would probably have decided to leave me behind if I'd started to argue. Better to go and get a night's sleep, or practise sitting with knees drawn up to chin. Elijah was putting on weight by the minute, and by now he was twice his original height. How was anyone, particularly anyone as small as Sue, going to be able to drive him?

We left shortly after dawn. In the discreet lanes of Mercedes and Bentleys queueing for embarkation at Dover, Elijah stood out like a vulgar defiance, and entire car-loads passed us by, gawping freely. We sat tight, ignoring the scrutiny, or returning stare for stare as the fancy took us. We had no option but to stay there, as we could not go aboard until the last because of our huge, unwieldy shape. I began to think the port authorities might refuse to take us. In fact, I was already so uncomfortable that I rather hoped they would.

With our arrival at Ostend, the relatively normal part of the journey was over. After that we drove almost non-stop through Belgium and Germany till we seemed to come to a halt at the German-Czech frontier. The Czechs did not respect our haste, nor were they impressed by Elijah. They were distinctly suspicious of his monstrous bulk, in spite of our presenting a sheaf of imposing letters with big red seals from the Polish and other Embassies in London, authorising us to proceed. We were left to cool our heels while the border guards decided what to do with us, or until they had received instructions from on high. What caused their change of heart we never discovered, but suddenly they were all round us, wreathed in smiles and urging us forward with benedictions. They did, however, take the precaution of sealing up the van at the back, forbidding us to open it again while in transit through their country.

Elijah, liberated, began to eat up the miles to Prague. As I remember only too well, that was the only eating that was done, apart from a lone banana on the shores of a lake where we stopped to wash off the grime. As we drew near the outskirts of Prague, I promised myself that as soon as we reached the city, we'd be stopping for a meal. No such luck. As we drove out of Prague again, I began to be obsessed by the idea of food. Mile by mile I dwelt on the prospect, sighting possible restaurants with hope, sighing as we left them behind. At last, halleluia, we stopped at an inn of some kind, went inside, and found that it sold only sausage. That was fine by me, but I had forgotten it was Friday, still at that time a day when Catholics were forbidden to eat meat. Sue wouldn't stay, and I, to whom the sausage seemed more desirable just then than Lobster Thermidor, and who would have agreed to burn in hell for the chance of a plateful, followed her sulkily outside. It must have been about two hours later, when night had already fallen, that we stopped outside a village tavern. By that time I was past hunger, and could manage only a bowl of soup.

We drove on towards Poland, then, when we were not far from the frontier, we slept for a little while, propped up in the van, with an alarm clock placed between us, ticking its way to zero hour. My rebellious stomach protested throughout the night like an erupting volcano, and sleep was fitful. By morning my ankles had developed acute elephantiasis. Sue was unsympathetic. 'You ought to be with me in winter', was her only comment. She has crossed mountain passes in fierce blizzards and force-nine gales, and she has come within centimetres of death on ice-bound roads. The summer, she could not help implying, was only for softies. This particular 140lb weakling was obviously being tried and found wanting.

We crossed into Poland at dawn – a beautiful crimson dawn rising over the Beskids in Southern Silesia, and for a few perfect moments we stopped to enjoy it. We ate a banana each (I was beginning to loathe bananas) and brewed Nescafé from a kettle plugged into a socket specially installed on the dashboard. The interlude was short-lived. Not for us the long, restful contemplation of a roseate dawn. We had a deadline to meet in Wroclaw.

Wroclaw was not always Wroclaw. Once it belonged to Germany and was known as Breslau: it was part of the hotly-disputed Oder-Neisse territories taken from Germany and given to Poland after the war. Feelings still ran high, and rivers of ink continued to flow, but we were not concerned just then with international politics. Our immediate destination was a Home for Incurables, run by Polish nuns, for terminal patients with cancer.

As we drove into the courtyard of the Home, we were hot,

sticky, dusty, cramped, tired and famished. A young woman of twenty or so detached herself from the crowd of people waiting to greet us. She ran towards Elijah with arms flung wide, and, as Sue alighted, enfolded her in a massive bear hug, her face a broad beam of delight. Greetings over, she proceeded to a commando-type assault on Elijah, almost leaping onto his roof to strip it of parcels, boxes and trunks single-handed. Her energy was exhausting to watch.

'My God,' I thought sourly, 'what it is to be young and full of energy. *She* hasn't been travelling hundreds of miles, wedged into that black hole of a van for three days, with nothing but bananas to feed on.'

Quite right. She hadn't. Sue told me her story later. Her name was Malgosia (Margaret), and she was one amongst approximately one hundred and fifty six children who survived Auschwitz. She knows that she was born in Lwow and that her father was a regular soldier in the Polish army. She thinks she was a twin but she is not sure. When she was about three she and her mother were transported by cattle truck to Auschwitz. (She believes that her mother was caught helping Jewish children to escape.) When they arrived at the camp, her mother was immediately liquidated, but the three-year-old child was 'selected' for medical experiments by the SS doctors in the camp. Petrol was injected into her legs to induce osteomyelitis (a favoured treatment for the women prisoners) and, for reasons forever unknown, her internal organs were removed and put back in different positions. She survived, and when Auschwitz was liberated she was rescued by the Polish Red Cross and removed to a children's home.

When she entered the home, Malgosia was incontinent, suffered from a heart complaint, was unable to concentrate on anything at all, and had no interest in living. Her life was an unending series of long illnesses culminating in unsuccessful operations. A teacher who knew Malgosia at that time remembers what she was like: 'She had no-one, she couldn't even speak a word of Polish. She was just an unhappy scrap of a child who belonged nowhere.'

Sue Ryder had discovered her on one of her earliest visits to Poland, and immediately arranged for her to have medical treatment in London. She had already undergone surgery in Poland, but her condition was unchanged. Doctors at a London hospital agreed to have a look at her, and when they did so they agreed that Sue had not exaggerated her case. They operated on Malgosia without much hope, but the story had a happy ending. Almost incredibly, after three major operations, Malgosia was no longer incontinent, no longer bed-ridden, no longer apathetic. She was, in fact, on the way to becoming the noisy, strapping young woman I had so envied that morning. 'I was one of the lucky ones,' she says, without a hint of irony.

The more I saw of Malgosia, the more I marvelled. She wouldn't have had time for bitterness even if she'd been disposed to feel it. She had no energy to spare for recriminations or hatred. Although she lived alone in a tiny garret up four flights of stairs (no lift) in an ancient apartment block in Wroclaw, she was actually, positively, shiningly happy. Her health allowed her to work for only a few hours a day, but she made the most of those few hours. She helped the nuns in the Caritas Home where we had met her, and quite clearly she was not only deeply loved but indispensable there; and on two days a week she became a social worker, for ZBOVID, a survivors' organisation, looking after children in a crèche. 'I must be with children,' she said. In her spare time, she did not take a well-deserved rest. She helped the Sue Ryder Foundation, collecting lost and stray survivors and finding out their needs — a deaf-aid, a bedpan, a wheel-chair, or perhaps a holiday. There was something very special about Malgosia, to which everyone she met seemed to respond.

The nuns who welcomed us at the Caritas Home took it for granted that we had had lunch (well, we had — two days ago) so they just gave us coffee. It was not till much later, when Sue was getting ready to drive off into the dusk, and I was beginning to think I'd never see food again, that Mother Superior walked in on our preparations, and invited us to supper. I could have thrown my arms around her neck. But Sue is made of sterner stuff, and hates taking food out of people's mouths. She began to protest that we could not stay. Hunger gave me the strength to resist her. More influenced by the thought of those blackening bananas awaiting us in the van than by the black looks Sue was giving me, I thanked the nun warmly and accepted her kind invitation. Now, at last I could let imagination run riot, savouring the taste of culinary delights to come. At supper-time I almost ran into the refectory — only to see a solitary boiled egg on each plate. 'It is such a pity that we cannot offer you more,' smiled the Mother Superior regretfully, 'but you see, today is the Vigil of the Feast of the Assumption of Our Lady, and it is a fast-day.' I might have known there'd be a catch. I could have wept.

We stayed in the Home that night, sleeping like logs on makeshift couches in the surgery, out for the count as soon as we hit the pillow. It was wonderful.

As we returned to Elijah next morning, I could see my square foot of seat was already occupied. 'Meet Pan Kowalski, a survivor of Buchenwald,' explained Sue. 'He's coming with us to help unload at the other end.'

'All the way?' I asked, looking a question at her.

'All the way,' she agreed cheerfully, climbing aboard. 'Well, don't just stand there, Mary, for heaven's sake. You can sit on a cushion between us, over the engine.'

We drove the one hundred and fifty kilometres to Zielona Gora like that, with me sitting on the hump, getting black and blue. Pan Kowalski was merely the harbinger. He was followed by scores of others. That square foot of plastic seat, which I had thought inadequate at the start of the journey, became a desirable luxury, mine by default when it wasn't taken over by an assortment of survivors of every camp under the sun. But bumping about between the gears and the hand-brake, I threw English stuffiness to the winds, and began to enjoy myself. Meeting these people, hearing their appalling stories, marvelling at their courage, I was lifted into a new world. What I had found at Cavendish had been no fluke. These people were characterised not only by courage and lack of bitterness, but also by an infectious gaiety and a child-like fun. Laughing with them, enjoying the absurdities of life with them, I was being given living proof that the human spirit was indestructible.

CHAPTER 9

Sue, Paul and a Party

As WE DREW up alongside a pavement in a side street in the centre of Warsaw, someone tapped on Elijah's window. When I opened it, a hand thrust in a bunch of flowers. Sue had prepared me; the Poles shower her with gifts: flowers (sometimes complete with vase and water), Polish chocolates, young trees, live chickens, and sundry other offerings. Once there had even been a large turkey. I blanched at the thought of sharing my metal perch with a furious barnyard fowl.

Within seconds, it seemed, the grapevine had got to work and borne fruit, and the whole of Warsaw knew that Sue had arrived. Survivors (and others, of all ages) appeared to come from nowhere, out of nooks, crannies or holes in the ground, like children answering the call of the Pied Piper. It was all beginning for Sue, and, for a few days, finishing for me. For her the coming week would hold an unending flurry of meetings with the Minister of Health, with the British Ambassador, with architects, painters, all manner of officials and local authority workers. There would be visits to the Sue Ryder Homes and to the local hospitals, and to housebound people, too sick to come to her.

For me, there was Paul.

He looked right through me, without the faintest idea of who

I was, though he was quite willing for me to hold his hand. On first glance he was not any different from when I had last seen him, but when I got used to seeing him again, it was obvious that he was a little taller, a little thinner, a little straighter. Best of all, he was a lot calmer, no longer dashing around like an aimless spinning-top. Dr W. was pleased with him. The adaptation period was now over, he said, and everything had gone as he had hoped. Even the chronic bronchial trouble seemed to have cleared up, and Paul was not wheezing any more. As he sat and watched the other children play ball, an angelic smile lighting up his face, I thought I had never seen him so happy.

It was a time for clutching at straws. 'A day to remember,' exults my diary for Friday, August 20th. On that day, I had again gone to the sanatorium outside Warsaw, this time with Basia, the friend with whom I was staying, and who was bilingual in Polish and English. (Her mother was an Englishwoman who had come to Poland after World War One.) Until then, language had been a problem. I spoke French fluently, but my German was halting and fractured, as well as inadequate. As few people at the hospital seemed to know French, our conversations were usually conducted in a bastard mixture of English, German, Latin and Polish. The result was that I was short on hard facts. With Basia present, I could at last hope for some real answers to my questions.

When we arrived, Paul was sitting on a bench in the sun with several other little boys, one of whom had an arm draped affectionately round him. Tears stung my eyes at the normality of it. It was the first time since the Training Centre days I had seen a child (apart from his brothers) go near Paul, let alone put an arm round him. The nurse in charge saw that the scene had affected me. Yes, she said, the other children were fond of Paul. 'He is a very lovable little boy,' she added. It was sweet music to my ears. Paul, said the nurse, knew the other children and responded to them. Whenever he heard the sound of their games outside his room, he would dash out, in his lumbering, bear-like way, to join in. I could scarcely believe it; it was more than I had ever dared hope for.

Watching the children have their mid-day meal, I was given

another welcome shock. Paul, whom we had always had to feed, spoonful by dreary spoonful, was now happily helping himself to gherkins, and later to apples and cake. He still couldn't manage the softer food, but his fingers could pick up and put down the more solid items. 'If he drops a piece of cake on the floor,' the nurse smiled, 'he picks it up and puts it in his mouth.' Hygiene be blowed, I was delighted to hear it. When he was at home, he would have been unaware of the dropped bits, and would simply have walked on them.

It was marvellous to see him adapting so well, and so patently happy. He was brown and fit too; the climate was suiting him. The fact that he did not know me from Eve, nor respond in any way to my voice, was something I had long ago trained myself to accept, as all of us at home had had to. What you have not had, and are not likely ever to have, is not worth sighing over. Not even communication with your own child.

Paul had come through the settling-in stage with flying colours. But what of the future? Dr W. was fairly sure that he could teach Paul to feed himself properly and even to overcome the chronic incontinence. But when I spoke to some of the medical staff later, they were much less sanguine. Paul, one of the doctors told me, was one of the most difficult cases in the whole sanatorium; he and his colleagues doubted that any more progress was possible.

For the time being, I was content to bask in Dr W.'s optimism, and to go and see one of his training programmes in practice. He had pioneered a summer camp not far from the hospital, persuading the Government to give him some land which had belonged to a former collective. (The policy of collectivisation met with little success among the fiercely independent Poles). It was rich farm land, bounded by a forest on one side and a river on the other, and on it Dr W. already had sixteen cows, one hundred pigs, and enough farm-produce to make the sanatorium self-supporting.

A group of children was under canvas when I arrived. They were all at the 'training' stage, children who had been brought to the hospital a year or so earlier, unable to talk, walk, or even sit up in a chair. Now they were doing all three. The week they

were spending at the camp represented Dr W.'s desire to bring
them into close contact with nature and the simple life. On the
previous night, someone had lit a bonfire. The children had never
seen fire before, and their immediate response was to shout and
sing and dance up and down with delight. None of them showed
the slightest sign of fear.

Living in the open, learning about the elements at close hand,
taking their turn in the queue leading to the communal cooking-
pot, they were being taught essential lessons about life, in the most
natural way possible. In an atmosphere like that, they could not
fail to improve.

Nearby, on the same terrain, a new building was going up.
Here the better-adapted among the children would spend an entire
year, working on the farm or in the fields, gardening or doing
simple carpentry, any jobs to which their small talents might be
stretched. And, at the end of it all, the pot of gold at the end of
the rainbow, the only reward that Dr W. dreamed of – the
possible return of his children to a normal life within the community.

That evening, when I got back to Warsaw (a two-hour journey
by bus), I found a message waiting from Sue. We were invited to
a party. The Poles love parties, and any excuse will do. They
don't need alcohol, they can get stoned on good will and high
spirits. Sue Ryder's visit was an opportunity not-to-be-missed, and

a gala night had been planned. Nothing loth, I found my way to the address I'd been given, and walked into a scene of chattering festivity, in which I was seized, greeted and smothered with sandwiches and questions. The guests were all women, dressed in their best clothes; and about half of them wore tattoos on their fore-arms. I knew that that meant Auschwitz. The others, I soon discovered, were survivors of Buchenwald and Ravensbrück, and the party was being given by the Survivors' clubs of those camps. For a moment, the evening took on a hint of the macabre, as I looked over that sea of young-old faces, every one of which had supped full with horror. It was grotesque, and I wasn't sure that I wanted to stay. Then there was a rustling and a sighing. Sue had arrived ('Mamusia', they call her, which means Mama). The faces glowed with anticipation. The evening could now begin.

It began, as did so much else, with flowers. Flowers for Sue, presents for her and even for myself, presented with much giggling and shuffling and hugs. Someone made a very Polish speech to the effect that we were welcome, not once, not twice, not three times, but a thousand and a hundred thousand times. Everyone cheered and then they burst into that rousing 'May you live a hundred years' song ('Sto Lat'), which is their equivalent of 'For she's a jolly good fellow', and without which no Polish gathering is complete. Poles always break into song, given the least chance, and they sing with a marvellous blend of melancholy and passion, which is tremendously moving.

One song led to another, and soon they were well away. Between singing and dancing and ruby-red barszcz, mushroom patties and tiny wild strawberries, the evening passed like a dream. There was much laughter. The astonishing thing was that a few of them could even talk about their experiences in the camps and laugh about them. On this evening at least, memories were not allowed to dim their gaiety.

Maria, a survivor of Ravensbrück, for example, told me in a matter-of-fact way about sleeping conditions at Ravensbrück camp — hundreds of women crammed into wooden bunks, stacked on top of each other. 'I dreamed the same dreams every

6

night,' she said, 'I dreamed of having a pillow, and of being by myself in a room of my own.' In all the filth and human misery, she had clung to her two dreams, longing for the privacy that might one day be hers. 'And, do you know,' she said with a smile, 'it never happened.' She got the pillow but the rest of the dream couldn't come true, because when at last she was released, her health had collapsed and she was unable to work. She lived with some distant relations, who provided for her basic needs; but they were so poor that they all had to sleep in the same room.

One woman at that party seemed to be hovering on the fringes, not joining in. She was the stranger at the feast, I thought, the only obviously unhappy person present. I was curious, and moved closer to her. She was eager enough to talk. She had come along because she wanted to meet Sue Ryder, from whom she wanted a favour for a friend. So far she hadn't been able to get near, because of the crush, but she hadn't given up hope. Then, without warning, she seemed to crumple. 'I wasn't there, you see,' she said, with real anguish in her voice. I looked at her in surprise, not understanding at all. 'I wasn't there,' she repeated heavily. 'Not in Auschwitz, not in Majdanek, not in Buchenwald, nor in any of those places. But I wish to God I *had* been. I'm on the outside. Can you understand?' The pain in her voice shook me.

Suddenly I knew exactly what she meant. The other women in the room were linked together indissolubly by a common bond of suffering, and by a mutual compassion. Somewhere in the depths of the hells they had lived through, bonds had been formed which could never be broken. They had been compelled to draw out of themselves almost impossible reserves of moral courage, and they had discovered an inner strength of such power that no amount of physical hardship or deprivation could touch it. Their humanity had been stripped of everything that was not essential to it; and they had found its rich distilled essence. They were special. If I had been Polish, I think I might have felt as this woman felt.

As it was, I could only marvel at their present happiness. As Sue and I left, they sang one of their heart-tearing songs by way of farewell. My own heart went out to them. I already knew what a lot I owed them.

CHAPTER IO

Wanda, Hanka and Others

IT IS DIFFICULT, and even invidious, to single out a few stories from among so many, but Wanda, Hanka and Professor Reicher will serve.

Wanda was a Girl Guide in Lublin during the Nazi occupation. She helped look after sick people, and from time to time she took secret messages to members of the Polish Resistance. One day, just after her seventeenth birthday, the Gestapo came to the house and arrested her. They took her to their headquarters in Lublin where she was beaten mercilessly. But they got no information from her. Then they threw her into a prison with prostitutes and criminals, a terrifying experience for a middle-class Girl Guide with a sheltered upbringing.

Much worse was to come. Before long, she was sent from there to Ravensbrück, the concentration camp for women, north of Berlin. She will never forget that long train journey, on which the women sang to keep up their spirits, and a strange comrade-ship sprang up among them. In the Polish part of the journey, villagers would throw scraps of food into the train as they passed. One of them threw a forlorn bunch of heather.

At Ravensbrück, Wanda discovered to what extent luck had deserted her, when she was sent to the medical experiment block.

Her legs were injected with petrol, and diseased bacilli were introduced into the bone marrow. Samples of muscle and bone tissue were taken away. All these details she discovered later. At the time, like the other terrified women in the block, she lay in fever for days, without any kind of post-operative care, not knowing what had been done to her or why. Some of the 'guinea-pigs' died. Wanda did not.

As the Liberating armies drew near, Ravensbrück's numbers were swollen to bursting point by an influx from other camps which had been hastily evacuated. Large numbers of men and women, for example, had been driven out of Auschwitz, on 'death marches' to other camps, to prevent discovery by the Russians who were approaching the camp. Only the very sick and the half-alive (many of them children) were left behind, as it was presumed that they would be dead by the time the Russians arrived. Of those sent on the death marches, many thousands perished; but some survived, to straggle into camps like Ravensbrück and add to the chaos already reigning there.

In Ravensbrück too the SS had laid their plans: the 'guinea-pigs' were to be liquidated, so that they would tell no tales. But there was an 'underground' movement within the camp, and in the prevailing chaos, they moved into action, their top priority being to save the 'guinea-pigs'. Wanda was among those constantly shifted from one dark underground bunker to another, hidden from the hourly searches made by the camp Gestapo.

One night she found herself lying side by side with a gipsy-girl of about fourteen. Even as she turned to look at her, the girl died.

When she saw this, Wanda was convinced that she too was dying, and thought how strange it was that this child of fourteen should have died before her, now an old woman of twenty-one. Suddenly she realised that she was past caring. The only thing that could touch her now was death, and that would be welcome. Even if the Gestapo caught her now, what could they do to her that they had not already done? Except kill her?

But strangely, as fear left her and she began to accept death as imminent, the conviction grew in her that she would not die. She would survive, because there was so much for her to do, when sanity returned to the world; and she fell to wondering what freedom would bring for those many women in the camp whose sanity had snapped under the intolerable pressures. And in the new calm which had possessed her, she determined that if she came out alive she would train to become a psychiatrist and strive to heal the minds that had been unhinged by a surfeit of suffering.

She was as good as her vow. Though she is frequently ill herself, and her legs bear the scars of those ghastly experiments, she has put her entire experience to good use. She works now as a psychiatrist in the south of Poland, among the endless streams of mentally ill survivors, many of them unfortunately turned criminal. 'With her direct gaze and piercing blue eyes,' says a friend, 'Wanda was made for the work she is doing. She's the sort of person who can look at another and know what is going on in that other's mind.'

Wanda has worked with great compassion and understanding among the children who survived Auschwitz (even children who survived other camps were known generically as 'the Auschwitz children'), charting their development as they grew into adulthood, trying to counter the nervous instability and lack of trust which characterised so many of them. A few years ago, she published a book of short stories based on her experience of these children. In one of these haunting stories, a little boy, Antek, was fostered by loving 'parents' but remained withdrawn, secretive, never known to laugh. They played games with him, gave him toys, told him stories, but they could never raise so much as a smile. Then one day he went to sit with an old man, a neighbour, who was dying. Faithfully, he went back day after day. He seemed very fond of the old man. Then the old man died, and suddenly the boy began to laugh. The mother glanced in astonishment at him. 'Perhaps he is abnormal after all,' she thought.

> The boy sat staring in wonder at the old man. His mother tried to lead him outside, but the boy pulled her towards the bed where the old man lay. He stood beside it smiling. It was the first time she had seen him smile. She was astonished and embarrassed and tried to pull him away.

But the little one suddenly turned to her and said in an excited, breathless, childish whisper: 'Tell me, tell me, is it true, can somebody really die like that? Just ordinarily like that? Can someone really die without being killed?'

When she told me the story many years later, the woman still had tears in her eyes. She added: 'From then on, he started to laugh.'*

Hanka, a tireless worker for the Sue Ryder Foundation, whom everyone I knew seemed to call Pani (i.e. Mrs) Hanka, was married, with a two-year-old son, and living in Warsaw when the Germans overran the country. Her sister, but not Hanka herself, joined the Polish Resistance, and eventually came under suspicion. When the Gestapo came to make an arrest, Hanka, who was living in the house at the time, passed herself off as her sister, believing that, as she obviously knew nothing of any value, the Gestapo would soon let her go. It was a naïve hope.

She was taken to the Aleja Szucha, the dreaded Gestapo HQ in the centre of Warsaw. Even to-day, Poles can't walk past the building without a shudder although the name of the street has been changed. On the wall of one of the underground cells one can still read the words scratched by a wretched captive: 'It is easy to talk about Poland. It is harder to work for her, harder still to die for her, but hardest of all to suffer for her.'

Hanka was incarcerated underground in the Aleja Szucha for six months, and during that time was subjected to constant interrogation and beatings. When the Gestapo could get nothing out of her, they sent her to the infamous camp at Majdanek, where she became a block 'mother', renowned for her kindness and practicality. Those who were in the camp with her still talk with admiration of the help she gave them. She was the practical one, to whom they all turned.

But Hanka's own memories are more sinister. For a time, she was made to separate the newly-arrived mothers from their chil-

* From a collection of true short stories, *Stare Rachunki* by Wanda Poltawska. Published in Poland and translated (unpublished) by Jessica Gatty.

dren, under threat that, if she refused, the guard dogs would be let loose to do the job more thoroughly. As it was, the children, she knew, would go straight to their deaths, the mothers later, when they had outlived their usefulness. 'All I could do,' she says, her face ashen at the recollection, 'was try and inject some humanity into the agonising task, but no amount of kindness could make any difference. How could it have? The faces of those poor children, their screams of terror, the anguish of the mothers, will haunt me to the grave. I wake every night, sweating and screaming, and the nightmare is always the same one.'

Poland is hag-ridden with memories of that sort, images of horror that refuse to go away. It is surprising that mental illness is not rife, the fruit of experiences which no words could describe. My own friend, Basia, is still haunted by the memory of an old Jew bending down in the street to fasten a shoe-lace, and being hauled to his feet by a passing SS man who proceeded to beat the old man's brains out against a lamp-post.

But most people do their best to put memories like that behind them and to live in the present. Like the woman I saw in a Home for terminal cancer patients just outside Warsaw. I have a photograph of her, but even without this constant reminder, I would be unable to forget her. She was sitting up in bed wearing an old-fashioned, buttoned-up-to-the-neck, snowy-white night-gown, with a white kerchief on her head. Her eyes were button-bright. Her husband, she told me, had disappeared in Auschwitz, her sons had been killed in the Warsaw Rising. She and her daughter had survived the siege, but during it the daughter had become severely crippled. They had scraped along as best they could since the war, but now she was dying of cancer. 'I am so lucky,' she kept saying. 'I have a room to myself, and it has curtains at the windows. Look how pretty the curtains are. And I have food brought to me three times a day. I think I am already in Heaven.'

I grew used to meeting people like her. In the Sue Ryder Home in Gdynia (which has since become a treatment-centre for men, women and children with cancer), I met three women with terminal cancer. They knew they had not long to live, but the agony of that knowledge had been offset by their joy at being given a place in this Home. A weight had been miraculously lifted from them, they said. 'I shall be able to die in peace now,' one of them said quite calmly. 'I feel so very happy.' Her companions nodded agreement. 'It's the English mattresses,' said one of them, by way of explaining the inexplicable. 'You cannot imagine what a difference they make.'

Professor Eleanora Reicher was Jewish. She was one of the handful of men and women who survived the liquidation of the Jewish community in Poland. Throughout the Nazi occupation she remained hidden in a Catholic convent, but she never stopped working as a doctor. She was one of Sue's earliest contacts in Warsaw, and she shared with the young English-woman her own dream of setting up a Home for the large numbers of post-war children, born with rheumatic arthritis and living in difficult conditions all over the country. With Sue Ryder's help, Dr Reicher's dream came true. Fourteen miles out of Warsaw, in the health-resort of Konstancin, two simple Homes were built by the Sue Ryder Foundation amid the pine forests. Here in these near-idyllic surroundings fifty or sixty severely crippled girls were admitted, not only to receive medical attention, but also to study for examinations, a possibility not open to them in the conditions in which they had been living at home. Of all the Homes she has established in Poland, this one in particular is home to Sue on her journeys. Konstancin is the Polish equivalent of Cavendish, the place where she feels most completely at home, and where she is always assured of a most ecstatic welcome. As soon as her van is sighted, girls of all ages set off walking or hobbling on crutches towards it, putting all they have into the effort. Amid the excitement and the expectant laughter, it is easy to forget for a moment that the girls are often in great pain, and that many of them will be disabled for the rest of their lives. But then, that sort of thing always seems secondary in Poland.

CHAPTER II

The End of the Journey

NOT ALL THE Sue Ryder Homes were conveniently near to Warsaw. Many of them were far away. Homes and Centres for the dying and the chronic sick merged indistinguishably in my consciousness during the long drives to the north, south, east and west of Poland. Fleeting images remain: passing hay-carts, waddling ducks and gaggles of slow-moving geese in the sunshine one day, and the next nearly skidding over a dead cow lying across a wet road in the eastern forests; pitying the unfortunate peasants huddled under sheets of newspaper or sodden tarpaulins while their animals wandered dispiritedly all over the road; crossing the Vistula one night on a slippery, makeshift bridge; and being diverted one dark evening through a forest in central Poland, watching Elijah's headlights illuminate the trunks of ageless trees, to the magical accompaniment of Bruch's No. 1 Violin Concerto on the radio. From Poznan in the west, south to Cracow and the Carpathian mountains, to Radom in the centre, over the flat Warsaw plain, east to Bialystok, then north to the lake-land of Masuria and what had once been Eastern Prussia. Night and day blurred into one, and I could not remember that far-distant time when I did not spend every night sleeping upright in an Austin van.

Hospitality was frequently offered us by friendly villagers and farmers, but we always refused because of lack of time. Sue would drive until she felt tired and then stop. (She had been driving for too long not to realise the stupidity of continuing to do so in a state of exhaustion.) When that moment arrived, she would bow to the inevitable and get out her small alarm clock. 'Three hours then,' she would say, somewhere in night's blackness when I had long been bleary with sleep. Down went the clock between us, ticking away inexorably, while we wriggled and turned and vainly counted sheep. No sooner did we drop asleep than the alarm dragged us relentlessly awake, to rub the sleep from our eyes and be on our way once more.

Some places are unforgettable. Treblinka, for example. It was a glorious day, the sky was a radiant blue, and it was hard to believe that in this peaceful setting over eight hundred thousand Jews and other victims had been murdered. Treblinka was not even a labour camp; it existed for one purpose only — extermination. Suddenly to come upon the memorial to the dead at Treblinka is a heart-piercing experience. I don't know what I was expecting. Perhaps a vast imposing sculpture and a flood of propaganda. The reality was a simple mound of stones surmounted by a fresco, while all around great jagged rocks thrust upwards as if in supplication, each bearing the names of towns or villages throughout Poland whose sons and daughters had ended their lives in this place. I was glad of the awesome silence, the solitude, the almost tangible need for prayer. A place of pilgrimage indeed.

Not far from Treblinka, we stopped at a rambling convent where a small band of devoted Benedictine nuns looked after eighty mentally-handicapped boys, without benefit of running water. They worked on a rota system, drawing the water they needed for drinking, cooking and washing from a nearby well. Knowing only too well the washing problems inherent in the care of the mentally handicapped, I was aghast at the difficulties under which the nuns were labouring.

And there was Radom, a town in central Poland where Sue was hoping to build a Home for men and women suffering from different disabilities. Many of these were single, and although until recently they had been able to work, they could do so no longer; others had lost their entire families and had nobody to care for them. Sue's Home was to be built as an annexe to an already-existing one, run by Sisters of Charity and over-crowded. I imagine Bedlam to have been something like it. Outside in the sunlight a woman was knitting — with one arm. The other hung, withered and useless, by her side. An impossible feat, but there she was, performing it with great skill and dexterity. When we had finished admiring her work, Sue went off to talk to the patients on the ground floor, suggesting that I might do likewise with those upstairs. I did my best, but it was her they wanted, not me. Apart from that fact, language was a terrible obstacle; I had to summon every word of Polish in my scanty vocabulary, and strain to catch at least the gist of what was being said. In the end some sort of rapport must have been established, as I have a vivid recollection of an old blind woman bursting into tears and throwing herself into my arms. And when that happens you don't need words.

On the night before we were due to leave for England, the streams of people arriving to make last-minute requests to Sue stretched on towards dawn and beyond. Next morning about thirty of the 'Bods' were on her doorstep to say goodbye, armed with biscuits, flowers, chocolates, sandwiches, vitamin pills, medical prescriptions, good advice and tears. They are always quite sure that if they don't provision her she will die of starvation on the way home. Remembering our own outward journey, they could well be right.

We could not leave immediately though. Sue had to get some more sleep before she could contemplate the long return journey – even though she almost knew it by heart. At 2 am the following day, she came to collect me from Basia's flat, and we slipped quietly away towards Katowice.

The name didn't really register at first, amid so many strange Polish names that I had grown used to. We were nearly there when I remembered. Katowice was near neighbour to Oswiecim, and Oswiecim was better known as Auschwitz. I wasn't sure that I could take Auschwitz, but I was quite sure Sue would make me try. She did.

Pan Tadeusz Szymanski, the curator of Auschwitz, and Pani Odi, his assistant, were both survivors of the camp who went on living there (in what was now a museum) because they believed they had a sacred duty to do so! Sue left me in their charge, while she drove off to visit a Home some miles away. Mr Szymanski, I learned, spent most of his spare time trying to unite the former child-prisoners of Auschwitz with their parents. A few weeks earlier he had managed to reunite a Russian boy, now aged twenty-eight, with his mother in Russia. A happy ending? Not entirely. The boy (after years of living in Poland) could speak no Russian, and the mother no Polish. There were many grave problems of that kind in Mr Szymanski's self-imposed task; the long hoped-for reunion often caused more problems than it solved. But he still felt he had to go on working to reunite parents with their long-lost children.

It is surely not possible to visit Auschwitz and be unaware of evil. Viscous and fetid, it is everywhere. It seeps into the pores, it is part of the air you have to breathe. From the moment I walked through those gates whose cynical legend still boasts: Arbeit Macht Frei (work sets you free), I was almost overcome with nausea. Standing in the museum with its vast glass cases filled with the macabre evidence of the wholesale slaughter of the innocents, I was near to fainting. It was unbearable to see the mountain of shorn human hair, the piles of false teeth, spectacles, clothing; the pathetic heaps of human trivia which the victims had brought with them, believing they were going to a resettle-ment camp: suitcases, cooking utensils, chamber-pots, walking-sticks, shopping-bags. Most poignant of all — the wooden legs, children's teddy-bears and family photographs. The intolerable pathos of little things. And in the main hall the flags of forty different countries recalled the homelands of the four million who came to this infamous place to die.

Auschwitz is a silent place where words are not only unneces-sary but impossible. You do not speak here, you choke back the tears. You stand and look at the innocuous railway-siding, re-membering the cattle-loads of human beings that once were shunted there, to be disgorged with shouts and kicks. Nearby, the remains of the crematoria, hastily but not completely des-troyed in the last days of the camp, still bear a mute, appalling witness. And beyond, the fields, the unhealthy tracts of marshland where the ashes of four million human persons were scattered. Kneel down and pick up a handful of earth, and as the wet mud silts away, see the tiny, unmistakable fragments of human bone.

Words could never convey the effect of Auschwitz. It is a searing of the soul. It leaves you stricken, bewildered, convulsed with anger, terror, pity, grief, and a violent desire to be sick. Mentally and physically I felt pulverised, and the sense of night-mare was increased when I was led to a former SS cell, where Sue and I had been given beds for the night. But Sue did not come. The minutes became hours, and still there was no sign of her. I was convinced that she had met with a fatal accident, and won-dered in a panic how to word the telegram I should have to send to Leonard, if that were indeed the case. In the event I was very nearly right. Just before midnight, she arrived, pale and exhausted. Short of time, she had decided to ignore one of the ubiquitous Diversion signs (these often meant a detour of up to forty miles, nearly drove us berserk with irritation and usually seemed quite unnecessary). Suddenly she had found herself teetering on the edge of a precipice. By some miracle, she had righted herself, but she was badly shaken. 'Funny thing,' she said, before flaking out like a light, 'when I thought I was going to die, all I could think of was that I wished you were with me.'

We had a couple of hours' sleep in that grisly cell, and at just after 2 am we were on the road once again. As the Warsaw 'Bods' had done, Mr Szymanski sent us off well provided with flowers, sandwiches and flasks of tea. Mercifully, nobody gave us bananas. But then, that would have been impossible, since there were none to be had in Poland.

Auschwitz wasn't quite the end of the journey. There was work to be done on the return journey through Czechoslovakia, visiting the relatives of men who were still imprisoned in Germany, surely the most forgotten men in the world, and the most hopeless. Deported to slave labour and other camps in Germany at the outset of war, they had survived, half-starved and desperate. Released from the camps, they found themselves in a chaotic alien world, which held no place for them. Perhaps in a desire for revenge, or perhaps merely in order to stay alive, they had committed various crimes, ranging from petty theft to murder. Retribution was swift and certain, the sentences savage and, middle-aged now, they had not seen their families for more than twenty years. (Some of the men, of course, no longer had any family.)

I knew that Sue spent a great deal of her time visiting prisons in Germany, but it was only now that I realised the full poignancy of the situation. Meeting wives, mothers, and even grandmothers, I could understand at last, as never before, the full horror of a war which, twenty years after it had officially ended, was still casting its dark shadow of suffering.

Most of the women we saw were in Prague, but not all. On our last night, we drove to a small village outside Pilsen, had a brief sleep in the van, and set about looking for the final address on our list. At the inhuman hour of three in the morning we were prowling around looking and feeling like burglars. Hopefully Sue shone a torch on a lighted window, and I cringed, waiting for a torrent of abuse or a bucketful of cold water. But the face which appeared at the window was friendly and we got the directions we needed. We drove on and a few minutes later Sue

was parking Elijah outside a large apartment block where everything was dark apart from one lighted window. I sat back, prepared to wait. Sue looked at the window speculatively, then at
me. 'Well?' she asked.

'Well, what?' I already half-suspected what was coming next.

'What about you going up there? Someone's bound to know
the woman we're looking for.'

'Please,' she added. She knew I'd have to do it.

Unnerved at the thought of the hour, the strangeness, my own
inability to say so much as hello in Czech, I was even more unnerved by the prospect of being called chicken if I refused. So,
taking a deep breath and muttering a fervent prayer, I uncurled
myself from Elijah and entered the dark apartment house. I went
on climbing the stairs until I saw a shaft of light underneath a
door, and then nervously pressed the bell. If whoever answered
my summons had turned nasty, I was quite prepared to run, but,
to my amazement, I was greeted without surprise and with
polite friendliness. My garbled German managed to elicit the information we wanted, and with a sigh of relief I fled down the
stairs reflecting on the probable reception I'd have met in England
if paying social calls at such an uncivil hour.

All was well in the end. We found the woman we were looking
for, and she was so excited and happy with the messages we
brought from her prisoner-son that I realised how little it mattered that the hour was unsuitable. She made us welcome, and
hope shone in her eyes as she looked at Sue and listened to news
about a sad middle-aged man in Germany whom she had last
seen twenty-five years before, when he was nineteen. Always
she hoped that one day he would come home.

After that, we did a hell-for-leather dash for Ostend, almost
non-stop for eight hundred miles. Towards the end of this mara-
thon stint, even Sue was flagging. 'Can't you sing or tell me a
funny story or something?' she asked irritably. As I didn't deign
to reply (I was far too tired), she looked at me suspiciously. 'You're
not going to grumble, Mary, are you?' she pleaded. 'I couldn't
bear it.' I asked her what she usually did when she reached
exhaustion-point. 'Oh, I go into a field and scream my head off,'

she replied, 'but there's no time for that to-night.' As for the
reason why she went on putting up with the discomforts of
journeys like this, I knew the answer to that one. She had, in fact,
once told me, but I hadn't needed to be told, because it was the
only possible explanation. 'I think of the survivors and what they
endured. I could never have stood that, but somehow one has to
try and measure up to their courage.'

Sue had set herself a lifetime's task. 'As long as I am alive, my
work is to try and relieve suffering,' she had once said. And in the
prayer which she and Leonard had composed, and which hung
in the chapel at Cavendish, lay the secret of what guided them
both:

> . . . Grant peace and eternal rest to all the departed, but
> especially to the millions known and unknown who died as
> prisoners in many lands, victims of the hatred and cruelty of
> man. May the example of their suffering and courage draw
> us closer to Thee through Thine own agony and passion,
> and thus strengthen us in our desire to serve Thee in the sick,
> the unwanted and the dying wherever we may find them.
> Give us the grace so to spend ourselves for those who are
> still alive, that we may prove most truly that we have not
> forgotten those who died.

When the young Sue Ryder had first arrived in Poland, she was
caught up in the struggles of the Polish people to rebuild their
shattered country. The English girl's selfless determination to help
galvanised many of those who had been standing on the sidelines.
My friend, Basia, one of Sue's earliest helpers, was one of these.
Basia was no stranger to suffering. Her husband, Ryszard, had
been arrested and sent to a concentration camp in Germany a few
weeks after their marriage; and in the first year of the Occupation
her young brother Tadeusz was shot dead in one of the frequent
sporadic street round-ups. (When the news of Tadeusz's death was
broken to his mother, she burst into tears and said 'I suppose I
must thank God he cannot now be sent to Auschwitz.') When
the war was over and Ryszard had returned, Basia had preferred

to close her eyes to the misery all around her. 'Before Sue came,' she said, 'there were many of us who knew all about the problems of the chronic sick and their terrible struggle to survive. But there were so *many* problems. In every city and town people were clearing away rubble with their bare hands before rebuilding could start. With so much destruction and misery everywhere we turned, some of us felt paralysed. It was Sue who made the difference. She was full of compassion and afraid of no-one. Somehow she showed us what could be done. She opened our eyes, and that was when we found our courage again.'

It was two-way traffic, of course. The miracle was that the survivors, in being helped, gave so much in return. They had learned lessons about human values which only those who had lived with death could have learned. They had gained an extra dimension because they had learned what was important in life and what was not, and because, in their own daily lives, they were passing on that lesson. Perhaps, in the world's terms, they were abject failures, every one of them — sick, poor, unable to work, with a life that was going nowhere. But as I left Poland, I knew that they were rich beyond measure. And I envied their wholeness, if not the paths by which they had come to it.

CHAPTER 12

A Death in the Family

I HAD NOT been home very long when I received a long letter from an Auschwitz survivor called Stefan. Stefan's wife, who had been in Ravensbrück, had died after the birth of her second child in 1952. Stefan's own health was failing rapidly, and he was trying not to think about the day when he would be forced to stop working. Most Poles in those days took two jobs in order to make ends meet. If Stefan lost his one and only job, he would be in serious trouble.

The letter told me that the blow had fallen. His health had given up. For years he had dreaded this moment, and he knew just how bleak his future prospects were. 'I worry most of all,' said the letter, 'about the children. What will they become?' Having written those words, he must have stopped to reflect on what he had written, for he crossed out the last sentence and wrote: 'No, I must not worry about them. They are in God's hands, and there is only one important thing for them. I hope they will learn to have compassion for others.'

The reflection knocked me sideways, and years later it still does. Suddenly all the accepted ambitions that parents have for their offspring, and that I had for Anthony and Mark, were reduced to size. Health, wealth, reputation, success, fame — where did these stand on any eternal scale of values? Stefan had stumbled on the pearl of great price. He had, as his wife had, suffered at the hands of men and women without compassion, and the effects of their cruelties would be with him till he died from them. Yet, in spite of it, or perhaps because of it, he had learned a secret of inestimable importance: that the strongest force in the world was love, and that to share this knowledge with one's children was the most precious gift one could make to them. In the concentration camps, when all other qualities went to the wall, only loving-kindness had counted. Cleverness, rank, talent were of no account. What kept the spark of humanity alive was compassion – one wounded, stricken human being reaching out to another.

Somehow Stefan's letter epitomised everything that the 'Bods' had come to stand for, at least in my eyes. Because they had lived with death, they had understood what was essential to life. Their values were the right way up.

I think this came home to me most clearly when I returned to England after my visit to Poland with Sue Ryder. We had been, for the space of a few weeks, with men and women who were materially poor, if not down-right poverty-stricken, and whose condition was unlikely to improve. Yet one was aware of them as a community bound together by past suffering and present caring. They helped each other, shared what little they had, laughed together, wept together. They wore their humanity like a blazon, proud, triumphant and unconquerable. Then we found ourselves back in the land of plenty, where every man was an island entire unto himself, where false gods multiplied, the rat race was the general goal, and no-one knew how to talk to anyone else, let alone share his loneliness and pain. Becoming aware of the fear and dissatisfaction underlying the prosperity was like being hit in the face with a wet sponge. 'I want to do my own thing' had the status of divine revelation; success, keeping-up-with-the-Joneses, seemed to occupy the nation exclusively. Big was beautiful, 'getting it made' was all that mattered. Failure was out of fashion, and inadequacy had to be swept under the carpet. Who cared?

Well, that was the way it seemed, and I honestly had not been thinking of making comparisons until they reared up and hit me. And when they did I felt an overpowering nostalgia for what we had lost, somewhere on the road to full and plenty. At what point did material plenty (desirable in itself) become a surfeit? At what point did it cease to promote human happiness, and begin to destroy it? I'd have given a lot to know.

All the same, I did not suspect that before a year was out I should be back in Poland.

Paul was not going to get better. In spite of his earlier optimism, Dr W. had hinted as much just before I left Poland. And in March of the following year, Sue had written to me from India: 'I had a long talk with Dr W. when I was in Warsaw. He feels you should know that there will never be any real improvement in Paul's condition, in spite of all his efforts.'

It was a disappointment, but hardly a very great surprise.

The telegram arrived one bitterly cold December afternoon, an unremarkable English-looking telegram in the customary buff envelope, with no outward sign that it had started out in Warsaw. At first I could hardly take it in. It read simply: CHILD DESPER-ATELY ILL. COME IMMEDIATELY.

The Polish Embassy in London arranged for me to collect a visa the following morning. By the next night I was in East Berlin, where our Warsaw-bound plane was grounded for twenty-four hours due to fog and ice. Fully two days after receiving the telegram, I rushed breathlessly into the sanatorium where Paul lay critically ill.

It was his ancient enemy, bronchitis. He lay there, breathing stertorously, a cylinder of oxygen by his bed in case of emergency. The immediate crisis had passed, and I was reminded of all the other crises which had come and gone before he came out to Poland. But a closer glance at Paul made me realise that this time would be different. He had gone into an obvious decline, and the shadow of death seemed to lie over him.

I knew that, if he was pronounced fit to travel, I should have to bring him back to England with me, even if it was only in order that he might die there. In any case, he had already used up his time in Poland. Two years was all he had gone for, and he had already exceeded that time.

For the next two days I shuttled between the Polish Ministry of Health, the British Embassy and the Lot airlines office, making arrangements for our journey back. Within a week it was all fixed. Paul was coming home, and God alone knew how we would manage.

Because I was terrified of what might happen to Paul in mid-flight, the return journey was a nightmare, although everybody concerned made it as easy as possible for us. Paul was a dead weight; and there was always the sheer physical difficulty of coping with his incontinence on a journey. The ambulance which brought us from the sanatorium was allowed onto the tarmac, right up to the plane steps. Paul was lifted out on a stretcher and, as the plane was less than half-full, we had a row of seats to ourselves. On one of these an oxygen cylinder lay ready. At Heathrow, where we made a brief stop, an ambulance took us to a private room where a nurse was waiting. And when we reached our home airport of Ringway, Frank was allowed to bring his car out to the plane.

So next morning, there they both were, Paul and Nicky, together under the same roof for the first time, and neither of them aware, even now, of the other's existence. We kept Paul downstairs, turning one of the reception rooms of our Edwardian house into a temporary bedroom. Although he was only ten, he no longer seemed like a child; he had become a chronic invalid, his heavy body no longer supported by his puny legs. He would never again be able to walk, and there was something in his eyes which suggested that life had become intolerable to him. Poor Paul, condemned for the rest of his life to a bed, and, even within that small confine, unable to move without help. It was a herculean task which confronted us.

We held a family conclave. My mother and Betty had come to stay for a while, knowing that Paul was coming home. Betty was a skilled nurse, but she was getting on for seventy, and Paul was a heavy nursing case, unable to help himself in any way. She would not be able to cope for long, however skilful she was. Then there were the other children. Had we the right to inflict this double burden on them? Anthony was twelve, Mark eight; they both had friends whom they wanted to bring home from school. The presence of Paul and the problems he presented would inevitably make a big difference to their lives, and might well prove insupportable. When our doctor came to see us, he did not mince words.

'You can't keep him at home,' he said. 'It wouldn't be fair to any of you.'

Agreeing with him, we arranged for Paul to go into a hospital about twenty miles away. But when the time came for him to go, we found that we simply couldn't bring ourselves to send him. It was as though we were sending him out to grass, to settle into being an animated cabbage in some vast general hospital. However little awareness of his surroundings Paul had, we felt sure that he would know he had been abandoned.

So yet another agonised discussion followed. We all felt sure that he was going to die, but had no means of knowing whether it would be sooner rather than later. If sooner, then we needn't hesitate. If later . . . It could have been a matter of days or weeks; it could also have been one of months or years. And we were not sure of our physical strength.

In the end, Betty and I worked things out between us, on a three-month trial basis. She would come over from St Helens each week from Monday to Friday, leaving me free to get out of the house and concentrate on part-time teaching, and the public speaking I was doing on behalf of the Sue Ryder Trust. On Friday she would go home, and I would take over. I had no experience of 'heavy' nursing, and I was scared to death. But I didn't like the alternative, so I had to set about learning.

Frank and I got through that first week-end by trial and error, emerging bloody but unbowed, with a mixture of relief and sadness. It was only too obvious that Paul was suffering. When I turned him over onto his side, sat him upright, dressed or undressed him, washed him, changed his pads, he whimpered. Sores were forming, his body was a burden to him. It seemed more than ever tragic that we were unable to communicate with him in any way, or provide him with any means of temporary escape. He couldn't talk, play, read, and he was too deaf to listen to music.

Nevertheless, when Betty came back on the Monday, I felt almost happy. A hurdle had been crossed. Next time would be easier, because I would have more confidence. We would manage somehow.

There was no next time. The following Friday morning, 10th February, we found Paul dead — on the floor by the side of his bed. The irony was that it was not the arch-enemy, bronchitis, which had done for him. He had fallen out of bed, and suffered a heart-attack. He was ten years old.

Before grief, before tears, before any real understanding took over, I was conscious of the one, solid thought: 'Thank God we did not send him away to die among strangers.' If we had sent him, just one week earlier, as we had intended, we should have been tormented with regret. It was bad enough as it was. He had died alone, in the dark, while the rest of the household slept. We could only hope that he had died quickly and mercifully.

I was in a vacuum of feeling. Shocked, numb, distressed, incredulous, emotionally worn-out, I went through the motions that Friday like a zombie. Mechanically answering the questions of doctor, undertaker, parish priest, I just as mechanically went into the kitchen and prepared a Cordon Bleu lunch. I have often looked back on this item of behaviour, and found it inexplicable. With the world falling about my ears, and for no reason that I have ever been able to fathom, I set about meticulously chopping herbs and choosing spices, making a wine sauce, and generally concocting a banquet for which none of us had the least appetite. Perhaps we all do unaccountable things when under stress.

What did we really feel when Paul died—this child of ours who had never even recognised us? I can only speak for myself, and admit to a confused complexity of emotions. I knew that Paul's death was a release for all of us, and there is no denying that I felt a deep thankfulness that this phase of my life was over. But I felt grief too, most probably for the loss of the child he might have been; and there was the even greater pain of believing that I had failed him. A kind of desolation swamped me for a time, and for nights on end I could do nothing but cry. It was a crying which had no rationale except in remorse, and in some odd way I felt I was not entitled to genuine grief. Our friends were so sure that Paul's death was an unqualified blessing that I felt guilty about the grief I felt for him. I knew that what hurt most in the general rejoicing was the assumption that Paul's life had been a useless irrelevance, a disaster best forgotten.

To me it did not seem like that. Yes, I was glad he was dead. But at the same time, I owed him an incalculable debt. If our value as human beings lies in what we do for each other, Paul had done a very great deal: he had, at the very least, opened the eyes of his mother to the suffering that was in the world, and had brought her to understand something of the redemptive force it was capable of generating. I had been broken, but I had been put together again, and I had met many who bore far more inspiring witness than I to the strength inherent in the mending process. What Paul had done for me was to challenge me to face up to the reality of my own situation; and he had handed me a key to unlock reserves buried so deep I hadn't suspected their existence.

Self-knowledge comes to us only in the dark times, when we are stripped of illusion and naked to truth. If Paul had helped me towards even a little understanding, how could I agree that he had lived to no purpose? He had taught me a lesson, quite unwittingly, and now that he was no longer there, I owed it to him not to forget.

CHAPTER 13

A Year-round
Christmas Gift

IT WAS FEBRUARY 1967 when Paul died and Anthony and Mark were thirteen and nine respectively. They were both bright, intelligent boys, who were very different from each other in temperament and skills. Anthony at that time was more withdrawn and academic, Mark much more of a carefree extrovert. Anthony was a potential mathematician almost from the cradle. To him Maths wasn't so much a school subject, it was a language, a philosophy, even a poetry. There was never any doubt about what he would become. In fact he eventually read for an Honours Degree in Mathematics and Computer Science and now, at twenty-four, works for a large international computer organisation. Even as a small boy, he read widely, particularly in history which, together with armchair sport, was an abiding interest.

Mark was much less keen on reading, except for books about wild animals, particularly snakes. Reptiles have been a life-long passion and he is at present spending six months working on a Snake Park and Crocodile Bank in Southern India, before going on to the university to read for a science degree in Psychology. Mark is a clever boy, but he has always felt in the shadow of his more academic older brother. He is much more of an all-rounder: good at languages and music and all kinds of sport. In his last year

at school he became Captain of Rugby Football as well as being a
very popular Head Boy.

Neither of them remembers very much about Paul or what it
was like when he was at home all the time. Anthony was ten
and Mark six when he went away to Poland. They were good
to him, but like everybody else they found it impossible to have
a real relationship with him or to get through to him at all.
Mark was the more patient of the two, but then I always felt
that the situation was much harder for Anthony, because he was
older. Paul had been part of Mark's world from the beginning,
but he had come into Anthony's world and disrupted it. And
how could a small boy understand that? There is no way of
knowing the damage Paul's presence may have done to Anthony.
Certainly it meant that he couldn't or wouldn't invite his friends
to the house. I think that he came to feel that, because of Paul, he
was different from other boys, and in time he began to resent it.
Perhaps for him Paul went away in the nick of time.

But Nicky, for both boys, was a very different matter. They
worshipped him from the start. From the first moment he came
home to us, Nicky was able to draw out reserves of patience,
tolerance and actual unselfishness in them both. As he grew older,
they often got mad with him, because he could be infuriating, but
on the whole they were phenomenally patient and understanding,
drawing him into whatever they were doing, teaching him new
words, games, songs, playing cricket with him. Nowadays when
they go away they send him picture postcards almost daily, and
spend hours choosing a toy that will be within his limited scope.
Whatever the drawbacks and difficulties, and in spite of the
regrets that he is not like other children, the presence of Nicky
among us has always brought out the very best in his two brothers.

'Don't expect too much too quickly,' warned the paediatrician, when Nicky was a small baby. 'He'll make progress, but it will be at his own speed, not yours.' Neither Frank nor I minded much about that, because something else this doctor had said had filled us with hope. There was no reason, he had said, why Nicky should not be able to talk. Perhaps not clearly nor very fluently, but there was nothing to stop him talking, in his own good time.

We both felt a tremendous relief at that welcome news, and we didn't mind how long we had to wait. Nicky had got off to a very slow start, having spent most of his first year in and out of hospital, and we should just have to wait for him to start catching up. We could afford to be patient. After our experience with Paul, Nicky's disabilities, severe as they were, seemed comparatively minor. It wouldn't be difficult to keep our sights low; for Paul they had had to be set even lower.

The first big break-through came when he was four. Until then he neither walked nor talked. But by the time he was four and a half, he was staggering around drunkenly on matchstick legs that were only just strong enough to support his weight. And his vocabulary was growing in great leaps. My mother used to spend hours (and so did I) singing nursery rhymes to him, and now we got our reward. Although he did not and does not have the faintest idea of tune, he started reciting them all, jumbled and garbled but quite recognisable. Baa baa black sheep was the all-time favourite, with Oh dear, what can the matter be? and something which always came out like ' 'ere we go ram the mummy push'. By the time he went to school (a special school for the mentally handicapped), he had such a large repertoire and was so proficient that he was selected to star in their Christmas concert for the parents. He was dressed as John Bull, in top hat, black suit and a Union Jack, and he sang Rool Bittamya with great gusto — until, like a fool, I stood up to take a flash photograph of him.

He recognised me, stopped in mid-phrase, and could not be persuaded to continue. I have never felt more like kicking myself.

He was less of a star at the school sports days when he usually either sat down when the whistle blew, or staggered off in the wrong direction. As he was given a balloon or some other toy as a consolation prize, he saw no need to make any great effort. In any case, he hadn't the slightest idea of what was expected of him. But success didn't matter to Nicky. He was blissfully happy at school, singing, dancing, playing with sand and water, making grey, sweaty pastry and banging the triangle in the percussion band.

We had moved from Hale to South London when Nicky was three. The move meant that Betty and my mother now lived far away, and I missed their help sorely. Obviously I was no longer free to go out and teach (which I was not really sorry about), or to continue giving talks for the Sue Ryder Foundation (which I regretted much more). Most meetings are held in the afternoon or evening, and I was once again house-bound at those times.

As I didn't see myself as either earth-mother or house-slave, I looked for something I could do in the mornings after all the boys had gone to school. The answer, surprisingly enough, was easy to find. I turned to free-lance journalism, and beyond it, to broadcasting – something I had always wanted to do, ever since I had first left university. I was lucky enough at this late stage to find an entrée. Interviewing, book-reviewing, feature-writing, mainly for the BBC's religious broadcasting department, but also quite often for magazine programmes such as *Woman's Hour* and *You and Yours*, I could fit in the dizzy whirl between 10 am and 2 pm, at which hour, like Cinderella, I had to leave the fun and make for home, in order to meet Nicky's school-bus at the end of our road.

It was a new world and I revelled in it. The restricted hours didn't really bother me, but all the same I was delighted when a group of nuns, Sisters of St Joseph, who lived in a small convent opposite us, offered to meet Nicky off the school bus on two days a week, and take him home for tea. Nicky adored them and quickly made them his abject slaves. He couldn't manage their real names, which were a bit difficult – Columcille, Regina, Ita, Reverend Mother. To him they were Colum, Jinga, Tar and Miller, while his beloved Sister Raymond, who made him special jellies and chicken sandwiches for his tea, became known to us all as Sister Ray Jelly. (The local parish priest who dropped in from time to time was Father God). The nuns kept tins of sweets and biscuits especially for him, turned on his favourite television programmes, and begged or borrowed children's records for him to listen to. He had his own place at their refectory table, and he knew the rules about meals. He would not let them forget about Grace, and when once he'd grasped that they often listened to readings from a selected book during mealtimes, he would go and get the current book out of the cupboard before the meal started and present it to Reverend Mother (Miller) saying: ' 'Ere's Jesus book. Read.'

From the moment he could walk, he proved to be as full of mischief as any normal toddler, hiding everything within reach. I would find apples in the washing-machine, screw-drivers in tea-pots, socks inside pillow-cases and the kettle-lid in the fridge. He was an opportunist. If I paused in the bed-time songs I used to sing after he was tucked up, he would open his eyes and ask hopefully: 'cuppa tea, cake?' And when once I dozed off in mid-song, he seized his chance, slipped out of bed and went to join the rest of the family round the television set. 'Richard Baker – nooz' he explained helpfully when I rushed downstairs to retrieve him.

Nowadays we live in the country, in a village in Berkshire, and he has had to make new friends. The children here find him a bit strange, and he's too shy and clumsy to join in their games. But he's happy to stay on the fringes and watch. The children are patient with him and keep an eye on him; and if they see him wandering too far they bring him back. We live in a U-shaped Close, and the neighbours have become used to periodic, unsolici-ted visits from Nicky. None of them seems to object. Nicky bestows his affections liberally on everyone he meets. One Sunday when we took him for a walk along the Kennet and Avon Canal, he ran up to every stranger like an exuberant puppy, saying hello and giving them a hug. His victims looked startled for a moment but they soon thawed under the unexpected onslaught and hugged him back.

Country life has few charms for Nicky, a born townee and lazy to boot. On the rare occasions when I take him for a walk through the woods at the back of our house, and over the adjoining common, he protests loudly and makes a great nuisance of himself, darting off down overgrown paths which lead nowhere, and having to be retrieved like an errant dog. ('I've been pickled,' he announces indignantly, picking the thorns out of his knees). It gets wearing. I gave up trying to make the walks educational after one occasion when I had been faithfully pointing out flora and fauna as we went along. We sloshed through thick mud in our wellington boots, trying to avoid the 'pickles', with Nicky trailing along ever more mutinously. Eventually we saw a horse in a field, and went to talk to it (or rather *I* did). In another corner of the same field were four donkeys. 'Look, darling, donkeys,' I enthused. Nicky ignored the donkeys and glowered at me. 'Bloody donkeys,' he muttered, 'bloody horse, bloody mud, bloody trees, bloody flowers.' Then he gave me a glare to end all glares — 'and bloody RICE PUDDING,' he thundered furiously. Having got all that off his chest, he recovered his good humour and was quite cheerful for the rest of the way home.

Not long ago we went on a touring holiday in the English Lake District. All attempts to interest Nicky in either new-born lambs or age-old mountains failing lamentably, we settled for the petrol stations which seemed to interest him much more. Though he resists anything which he feels might tax his brain, we taught him to identify them, and by the time we were homeward-bound he was an expert shouting out the names of Shell, Esso, Texaco, Burmah, BP and National before we had spotted the signs ourselves. Not much, as intellectual achievements go, but he was immensely proud of himself. 'Orl bah m'self,' he crowed, every time he scored a hit. Success even made him better disposed towards the cows and sheep in the fields, and he deigned to give them the odd glance as we passed. 'Cows give petrol,' he suggested with a glint in his eye. 'Sure, Nicky, remind me to give you a nice glass of petrol when we get home.' 'Na-ow,' he gurgled, doubled up at his own wit, and suddenly knowledgeable. 'Cows don't give petrol, cows give milk an' butter an' cheese an' meat.' But the possibility of a game had occurred to him. 'Pigs give eggs, an' hens give elephants', he chanted hopefully, giving us variations on this theme for the next few miles. It made a change from petrol stations.

Later, when this palled, he thought of something else. 'Mumps in me ear,' he said firmly, and looked at me for approval.

'What did you say? Come again.'

'Mumps in me ear, MUMPS IN ME EAR.' He was getting frustrated and irritable because he couldn't make me understand. It was only when he started: janulary, febually, march, that I realised he meant 'months of the year'. Then I knew what to expect. All such catalogues lead to 'Nobember' and Guy Fawkes Day (he doesn't bother with December, in spite of Christmas). 'NOBEMBER,' he yells in triumph, 'NOBEMBER THE PIFTH — farworks. Wockets.' He suits actions to words, and his joined hands shoot skywards in a great whoosh. Every year as Bonfire Night approaches his excitement grows, and we get more and more anxious-because the truth is that he hates fireworks. Two years ago we took him to a fireworks party, and as soon as he got there he covered his eyes and ears and asked when we were going home. Last year we tried having a few at home, with Frank and Mark setting them off, and Nicky watching from the sun-house. He kept pretending to cheer, but his terror was obvious. At intervals he would tell himself consolingly: 'Nebber mind. Soon be over. Better soon. Won't hurt,' — like a doctor trying to reassure a nervous patient.

Nicky is instantly at home anywhere and with anyone. 'Whass-your name? I'm Nicky,' he asks. He is completely trusting, believing that everyone he meets is a friend. No-one has ever given him reason to think otherwise, as he is a great charmer. When we had the outside of the house painted recently, he was a confounded nuisance to the painters, but they became firm friends. He adopted one of their phrases: 'Cheers, mite,' he greeted them each morning, with thumb extended from closed fist, and with a knowing wink.

But even though he takes universal good will for granted, he knows when appreciation is due. He and I were once invited to have lunch with an Earl at the House of Lords. Halfway through the meal (unimpressed by his august surroundings he had firmly ordered fish and chips and ice cream), he leaned forward and touched our noble host on the sleeve. 'Marbellous meal,' he murmured politely, 'nice, kind gentleman.' As we left, the peer fished in his pocket and gave Nicky a fifty-pence piece. 'Good lad, L——,' said Nicky, in tones of awed admiration. Though most of the time he is a thirteen-year-old scruff, his manners are impeccable when the occasion arises.

The big moments in his life are when he is allowed on to an escalator or into a lift. 'Escalator' was one of the first words to enter his vocabulary, and he never once got it wrong. When he went to Lourdes some years ago with a party of handicapped children, he went missing, and was eventually discovered happily going up and down in the hotel lift. ('What did you do in Lourdes, Nicky?' 'Went in lift.' 'And then what?' 'Got smacked.') Once when I was in hospital he was brought to see me, and was so excited by the lift that he hardly noticed me. 'Went to hoptible. Saw lift,' he replied when asked where he'd spent the afternoon.

His Saturday afternoon treat, which he talks about all week, is a visit with Frank to Newbury's one and only biggish store, where there is an up but not a down escalator. All the shop assistants in the store know him, and they wait for his gap-toothed grin to appear. When he gets to the top, he has to work his way through the shop, across the underwear department, and down some stairs. The first time he did this, as he walked amid the frilly things, his eye caught some objects familiar from his television viewing. 'Look', he exclaimed, in high excitement, and in a very loud voice, 'Playtex Cross-Your-Heart Bra, FOR A BETTER FIGURE.'

The television commercials have the attraction of constant repetition. He knows most of them by heart, repeating the text along with the voice-over, delivering the punch-line with all the hamminess of which he is capable, which is a great deal. Through them he has learned to read the brand names on grocery products, and he swoops on my shopping bag to identify them. 'BOVRIL', he announces happily, 'full of beefy goodness'. Or 'Oil of Oo-lay – makes my skin so nice and smooth'. He pats his cheek and drops his voice to an ecstatic whisper. His memory is excellent, and he does not forget what he has seen. 'Fly the flag,' he shouted excitedly, when we were on the motorway near Heathrow Airport. When I looked puzzled, he jumped up and down impatiently and pointed to a British Airways van just in front of us. 'Look. Fly The Flag,' he explained, adding with a smirk, in case I hadn't recognised the commercial, 'We Take Better Care Of You.'

Nicky is an out-and-out television fanatic. What he does at school (where he is very happy) is shrouded in mystery. When we ask him what he's been doing there, he says, 'Tomato pie and custard' or 'Carrots and ice cream' or even 'Mahnd yown bizness'. It's no use hoping that he'll wax more informative, because as soon as he reaches home, television is all he cares about. He sets about his hobby with considerable thoroughness. Every morning at breakfast he produces the Radio Times and TV Times and has two days' worth of programmes read to him. (If they can't be found, we have a crisis on our hands. He goes into a fearsome sulk, refuses all food, and is inconsolable. He can never be brought to understand that the loss is minor and temporary. To him it is major and devastating. Little things like this upset his equilibrium completely.) He listens carefully, assimilates what he has heard, and from then on he knows exactly who's on, what's on, where and when. And though he still cannot tell the time, except for the hour, he appears to have a built-in timepiece which tells him when to switch from one channel to another. (And if the colour on the set goes wrong, or the picture is otherwise distorted, he knows which button to press to put it to rights.) He likes most programmes, though he has his pet hates: Stars on Sunday, the early evening News summary, and Jackanory, during which he stalks outside the room and stands outside the door waiting for it to be over. He is passionately addicted to soap operas like Crossroads and Coronation Street; cartoons, especially Scooby Doo, have him rolling about the floor; and one year he sat through the entire Labour Party Conference with every sign of rapt attention.

8

Life with Nicky has its bitter moments — for one thing, he has had a lot of pain over the years — but it is a lot of fun too. He has the enviable gift of living in the present. When he's hurt or miserable, he howls or yells or sulks furiously. But he comes out of the misery with an engaging grin, like sunshine after storm, and all is completely forgotten. He has his own world of make-believe, a limited world which borrows its reality from others' actual experience. 'Right, I'll be off then,' he remarks purposefully donning anorak and shoes with great determination. 'Where are you going?' 'To the pub for a beer — to a party — to the folk-club — to a rehearsal — to play rugby — to the farm to see cows — to watch cricket,' he replies, according to his mood, in studied imitation of his brothers. (Once, in a burst of one-upmanship, he answered: 'to the House of Lords'). 'See you later,' he says breezily, and goes out by the front door, slamming it behind him. A minute later, he comes in again, by the back door. 'I'm back', he shouts, as though he's been gone for hours. We used to worry that he really would go off somewhere (and if ever he attempted to cross the main road at the top of the Close, he'd go right under a bus. He has not the faintest glimmering of road sense). But we now know that it is all a game, very necessary to his self-esteem and his own sense of identity. It doesn't seem to matter that none of it has any substance, that all of it is fantasy. He takes off his anorak, changes back into his slippers, and starts a long, highly realistic conversation on a toy telephone; or 'presents' a TV show, ('To-night, we are lucky enough to have . . .'); or runs through a DJ act, doing a count-down just like Tom Brown on Pick of the Pops, the only radio programme he ever listens to. He can always fill you in on the latest pop songs (as long as you can understand what he's telling you). As soon as he hears the first bar, he'll tell you the name of the song and the group singing it.

Although he is far from pious (despite an inexplicable and short-lived urge to sit at the piano each day, reciting the Lord's Prayer) Nicky rather enjoys going to church. Or rather, he likes the energetic bits, like going up to the Communion rail and singing hymns. When the time approaches for the Sign of Peace to be given, he gets quite excited, and as soon as he gets the go-ahead, he rushes round wringing the hand of everyone he can reach, with a beaming, 'Peace be with you, Mr Happy . . . Mr Bouncy . . . Mr Sneezy' after the pattern of one of his favourite TV programmes, Mr Men. 'Nicky's idea of the Sign of Peace,' commented a friend recently, 'is nearer the truth of it than that of most theologians.'

And when Mass is finished, he has been known to finish the recessional hymn with a resounding Boom, Boom; and most weeks he brings proceedings to a close with a discreet, sotto voce, 'That's it. That's all for this week, folks. Join us again next Sunday, same time, same place. Till then, cheerio.' He gabbles all this like an incantation, a mysterious ritual with which he cannot dispense.

The other great enthusiasm of Nicky's life is cricket. During the season he sits glued to the television set, refusing to come away even for meals. Avidly he follows every stroke, and when play is finished for the day, he solemnly collects his own bat, ball, wicket and stumps, and drags whoever is available out into the garden to play. He does a serious run-up with the ball, pausing to polish it professionally on his trousers, obviously lost in a Walter Mitty world, in which he is Gary Sobers and Ray Illing-worth rolled into one. When he's batting, his ambitions change: he is far more interested in hitting the ball over the garage roof or over the fence next door than in hitting a six.

Betty came to live with us when my mother died six years ago, and she is now an extraordinarily active eighty-four-year-old. Nicky adores her, regarding her as his own private property, a point of view which she is happy to share. The two of them live in a private world of mutual devotion, in the sort of harmony that exists between the very old and the very young. They share jokes and silly catch-phrases from her Yorkshire childhood which make them both giggle. Nicky teases her, calling her 'lovely man', 'nice boy', and occasionally he pulls a beret down on his face and does a Frank Spencer act. 'Mmmmm, Be-e-tty,' he spoofs, and they both fall about with delight. She is the heartbeat of Nicky's world, and when she goes away, even for just a weekend, he is bereft. He hates her to go out of his sight, and she is quite content that it should be so. 'Where she gone?' he demands, knowing very well that she's escaped upstairs to play a game of Patience. We are all very close to Nicky, but Betty is closest of all, since she is entirely his.

The future is hazy, and we cannot confront it yet. The biggest problem is likely to be Nicky's continuing incontinence. If it cannot be brought under control (and we do not see how it can be, unless he reverts to having a colostomy), we may find doors closed to him. And though none of us can bear the thought of being without him, sooner or later, for his own sake, we want to try and get him into some sort of community. A farming community, perhaps, such as those run by the Camphill Village Trust, or Care, or L'Arche — where he can learn to do simple, undemanding tasks while living in a fully supportive environment. If he goes on living with us at home as a mentally handicapped adult there will be the shadow which hangs over all parents of such people. What happens if one or the other parent dies? If both die? Rather than face the logic of that question we would prefer to ease him into a caring community, where he can build up other enduring ties of affection. It will be heart-breaking for us to make a decision about his future, but we shall have to decide what is best for *him*, long term, rather than take the short-term view, for ourselves.

Perhaps by the time we have to do our heart-searching, society will have come up with a few more answers to the eternal problem of the mentally-handicapped adult in its midst. Sheltered hostels would be the ideal. Nicky is blithely unaware that a question-mark overhangs his future. Though he is now a tall and apparently strong thirteen-year-old, in many ways he is still a baby, with a baby's need of protection.

We've kept our sights low, and Nicky's mental age does not seem all that important to us. What *is* important is the joy that he has brought us. He is the focal point of the family, the most beloved of every one of us. Not long ago a priest-journalist who is a close friend made him the subject of a Christmas reflection in the *Tablet*. Musing on the happiness and open affection which characterise so many handicapped children, he wrote:

No outsider like myself is in a position to dictate where the
limits of love lie, or to criticise those who find caring for
the handicapped an impossible burden. But it is astonishing
how often they draw out from others, especially their parents,
hidden reserves of patience and affection. How we treat
them seems to be in some wise our own and society's acid
test. In them, as in the Child of Bethlehem, we see, un-
camouflaged, the native value of humanity itself, helpless,
vulnerable, possessing nothing. And they have much else to
teach. They are fearless: they have no enemies. They are
trusting: their world includes no villains. They are loving:
they do not doubt themselves. They are the ghosts of our
lost innocence. Nicky will never build a car, or fly an aero-
plane, or balance a set of accounts. But he never stops
producing joy and love wherever he goes. He is a year-round
Christmas gift, however crumpled his wrapping.*

'I'm *glad* there was a Paul and a Nicky,' a friend of mine suddenly
burst out, a few weeks ago.

By and large, I think I am glad too.

*John Harriott: 'Periscope': *The Tablet* 18/25 December 1976.

CHAPTER 14

What Makes the Desert
Beautiful . . .

ONE DAY, ABOUT a year after Paul's death, I was asked to give a talk to a group of women about Suffering. I had to sit down and try and work out what I really did believe, try and impose some order on the jumbled rag-bag of ideas I had been assembling. It seemed impossible, but late one evening I suddenly found everything taking shape and assuming a coherence; and I rushed for a pen so as to capture the moment before it escaped me. I wrote far into the night, and was almost surprised next morning, when I read through what I had written, to find that it was as nearly authentic a summary as I would ever achieve, given my necessarily limited understanding. Everyone has to make his or her own terms with the suffering in his life. I had made mine.

The talk went down well. The women to whom I spoke obviously felt that here was something to which they could respond. The warmth of their response left me in no doubt that my conviction of the redemptive power of suffering was not something I had whistled out of the wind. It was a genuine human response, one which most people could illustrate from their own experience of life.

That was the first of many talks, articles, broadcasts. Too many for my peace of mind. I began to find it increasingly difficult. It wasn't so much the pain of remembering, but the fact of telling my experience over and over again began to empty it of significance, made it seem trite and commonplace. Also, in my determination to say only what I knew to be authentic and to avoid all hint of romanticism or self-pity, I was being emotionally drained.

I was feeling like this when the publishers asked me to write this book. Painful though it has been to write (and parts of it were so painful that if I hadn't forced myself to write them quickly I should never have written them at all) I've encouraged myself with the thought of the many people who have found the things I have previously said or written helpful. Perhaps this book will help a few others. Inevitably, though, it will offend those who deny that life has a pattern, and those who believe that to bring two children such as mine into the world is a heinous crime. (I have had one or two letters to that effect.)

In any case, I have reached the end, and what I have written here is intended as a post-lude to what has gone before, my final word on this subject. I shall give no more talks.

It is immensely difficult to say anything useful about a subject – suffering – which is at once so private and so painful. Even the lessons we learn can be learned only for a time, and then have to be learned all over again. Each fresh onslaught reduces us to jelly, and we have to wait for time to show us some kind of perspective. It's the same for all of us. One way or another, being broken up and put together again is the universal experience, the never-ending central drama of life. ('Man is born broken', wrote Eugene O'Neill, 'he lives by mending; the grace of God is glue') No-one can talk his way out of that basic fact about life, no-one can offer once-for-all solutions. There aren't any. My only excuse for wielding the pen in this delicate area is as one very ordinary human being who has discovered what many others have also discovered: that suffering can teach ordinary people some extra-ordinary things.

In the teeth of the evidence, I do not believe that any suffering is ultimately absurd or pointless. But it is often difficult to go on convincing oneself. When someone we love dies or meets with a violent accident, when a child is brutally murdered or dies of cancer, when a deep relationship is broken up, or when any disappointment or upheaval strikes, despair may set in. We are marooned in misery. Shaking our fists, pounding the air, we ask that despairing and futile question, why. Why, why, why? Most of all, why ME? What have I done to deserve it? If I were God, I wouldn't allow such awful things to happen. How can there be a God of love when the world is full of suffering? The very idea is a mockery. So we give ourselves two frightful alternatives: either God is cruel, unjust, without mercy, a super-being who delights in the affliction of his creatures; or there is no God and we are adrift in total absurdity, in uncharted and unchartable seas. It's a classic double-bind, a Catch-22 situation. Heads nobody wins, tails we all lose.

It's not really surprising, in a world which spawned Auschwitz, Hiroshima and Vietnam, and which seems now hell-bent on self-destruction, that so many have turned away from the mere idea of God, and from the possibility that life has a meaning and an underlying purpose. Job's 'I cry to you and you give me no answer; I stand before you but you take no notice' is not a cry for today, in the sense that there is no 'you', and the universe is believed to be empty. But today's cry is just as despairing, if not more so because there is nobody there to hear it. Any idea that good may come out of the evil we see, and that it may have a redemptive force we do not as yet comprehend, is a matter for scorn and derision, the pathetic bleating of a fool or a religious maniac.

Yet, isn't it at least possible that in the course of time all things do work together for good? In the concentration camp of Ravensbrück, that graveyard of so many human hopes and desires, an unknown prisoner wrote this prayer on a torn scrap of wrapping-paper, and left it by the body of a dead child:

O Lord, remember not only the men and women of good will, but also those of ill-will. But do not remember all the suffering they have inflicted on us; remember the fruits we have bought, thanks to this suffering — our comradeship, our loyalty, our humility, our courage, our generosity, the greatness of heart which has grown out of all this, and when

they come to judgement, let all the fruits which we have
borne be their forgiveness.

That prayer, with its white-hot humanity, seems to me to
proclaim and affirm the presence of God in the heart of the dark.
And if we dislike or are embarrassed by the word 'God', as so
many are, we can substitute another word or phrase — Love,
perhaps, or 'the one who *is*'. For myself, I had always clung to
Søren Kierkegaard's definition of the deity as 'the beyond in the
midst', but the playwright, Dennis Potter, has given an even more
satisfying one: '(God is) . . . someone present in the quick of
being . . ., in existence as it exists, in the fibre, in the pulse of the
world.'*

But if 'God' is the ultimate reality behind our world, it is men
who have been given the task of creating that world, inch by inch,
generation by generation, confronting the task every day of their
lives. We have been free — free to choose evil courses as well as
good. Free will, which is our glory, distinguishing us from the
animals, has also caused our sorrow. We needed no divine inter-
ference to turn our world upside down, to destroy our own
harmony and rhythmic at-one-ness with that world, to sow the
seeds of dissonance and discord. We could do it, did it, and
continue to do it ourselves through our greed, pride, ambition,
envy, blindness, stupidity and through the ignorance which we
can only gradually overcome. There is a fatal flaw in man which
makes his affairs go awry. (Theologians have called it original
sin, but the phrase is not a popular one to-day.) It is not God
but men who have made wars and devised ever more devastating
weapons of destruction or enslavement. Why should we blame
God for the concentration camps, or for the new and terrifying
concept of megadeath by radiation?

If God is present in our situation, surely it is as a guarantee of
continuing hope, of an eventual end to darkness, as the promise
that, in spite of present appearances, all will finally be well. It is

* The Other Side Of The Dark — Lent Talk by Dennis Potter,
Radio 4, March 1978.

precisely that hope that Christians find in Christ. The very heart
and core of the Christian faith is a man dying in pain and confusion
and shame, after his life has collapsed around him in total failure;
a man who cried out in genuine anguish a few moments before
he died on the Cross, 'My God, my God, why have you forsaken
me?' It has always seemed to me that, at that moment more than
at any other, Jesus was one with all the men and women who have
ever existed or ever will exist, sharing with them that sense of
abandonment, the desolating fear that their lives are without
meaning.

Yet Jesus's death on Calvary showed that despair, anguish,
emptiness and darkness were not the end of the story. What was
to all appearances a shameful death (that of a common felon), the
epitome of muddle and failed hopes, brought a new, confident
hope which rapidly spread throughout the world. Good Friday
is always followed by Easter Day, as surely as spring always
follows winter; and we continue to call it Good. The joy of
Easter is compounded of suffering and death *and* resurrection, each
element a vital one: despair followed by hope followed by
assurance.

To me the death of Jesus on the Cross demonstrates that self-
offering love is the only force in the world strong enough to
overcome death. Calvary is the greatest act of love the world has
ever witnessed, because it was a pledge of new hope and new life
from within the crucible of despair. 'If you refuse to love,' we
read in St John's Gospel, 'you will remain dead.' 'Caring is the
greatest thing', wrote the philosopher von Hügel, 'caring matters
most.'

But it is no use thinking that faith in the redemptive power
of the Cross is some sort of easy, comforting placebo. We shall
not find there a hole in which to shelter, a pious refuge from
the harsh onslaughts of reality. The Cross will not protect us
from pain, it will face us with it. Calvary challenges us (as does our
own personal suffering) to see ourselves as we are, in the situation
which is ours. It offers us the present moment in which to search
out and find the unsuspected reserves buried deep inside us. As
Léon Bloy once wrote, 'There are places in man's heart which do

not yet exist, and into them enters suffering, so that they may have existence.' Suffering is a key to the discovery of what we are, and what we have in us to become, if only we can summon the strength. 'What makes the desert beautiful,' reflected Saint-Exupéry's *Little Prince*, 'is that somewhere, far below its surface, it holds a spring of fresh water.'

The men and women I met at Cavendish and in Poland had discovered that life-giving spring. I don't need anyone to tell me that hopelessness and despair reigned in the concentration camps (just as they must reign in similar places today), that men suffered and died there without hope, that many were turned into raging beasts. Hatred and greed and the law of the jungle flourished. But everywhere there were the undeniable signs of grace – in the countless examples of self-sacrifice and compassion. There were heroes like Janusz Korczak, the Polish-Jewish doctor who refused all offers of a safe-conduct for himself and shepherded his orphanage children from the Warsaw Ghetto to the extermination camp at Treblinka, singing all the way; the Orthodox nun, Maria Skobtsova from Yugoslavia and the Polish priest Maximilian Kolbe, both of whom gave their own life as the price of another's; and Betsie ten Boom from Holland, who spread love around her in Ravensbrück, refusing to hate even the guards who beat her, and whose dying words to her sister Corrie were: 'We must tell people what we have learned here. We must tell them that there is no pit so deep that He is not deeper still.' *

Evil as they were, the Nazi concentration camps bore powerful witness to the human truth that, when the chips are well and truly down, the only thing that matters is the spirit. When the pressures were removed, the lesson was almost too painful to go on applying. In *The Real Enemy*, a moving account of his experiences in Buchenwald, Pierre d'Harcourt wrote with rare understanding:

> All I know is that when it became hardest of all for men to behave like decent human beings they spread their wings and rose to great heights; and when the strains and temptations were removed, they sank into the mud.

* *The Hiding Place*: Corrie ten Boom, Hodder and Stoughton.

In their heart of hearts they may have felt, as I did, that, in its way, it was the life of the camp that was the true life, the life that bore witness to what really counted in humanity, the Spirit . . .

This for me is the first lesson of the camp — that it made beasts of some men and saints of others. And the second lesson is that it is hard to predict who will be the saint and who the beast when the time of trial comes. Only one thing prevailed — strength of character. Cleverness, creativeness, learning, all went down; only real goodness survived.*

So the possibility persists that my friends, the survivors, have so much to teach us, *because* of what they endured rather than in spite of it. The value of suffering does not lie in the pain of it, which is morally neutral — but in what the sufferer makes of it. Two persons can go through the same painful experience, one be destroyed by it, the other achieve an extra dimension. The real tragedy of suffering is the wasted opportunity.

When disaster first makes its unwelcome appearance into our lives, self-pity is the first, unavoidable, normal and probably right reaction. Courage flies out at the window, the world seems all of a sudden hostile and menacing, an alien place where we are no longer at home. We feel as though we are falling apart, and are deaf to everything but the shriek of our own misery. In the early stages I don't see how it is possible to fight self-pity. We only exhaust ourselves in trying to keep it at bay. But there is a time limit, and we alone can fix it. I believe it is possible to recognise the point of no return, the moment when self-pity threatens to become malignant. And that is when we have to stand firm, for if once we allow it to get a real hold we are doomed. Self-pity is a cancer which erodes not only our courage and our will to happiness, but also our humanity and our capacity to love. It destroys us, and it destroys the friends who love us and who want to help. After all, if we come to see ourselves as the

* *The Real Enemy*: Pierre d'Harcourt, Longmans.

ill-used victims of outrageous fate, all our actions and thoughts will be governed by bitterness, rancour and sour envy.

It is like the moment that Jesus faced in the Garden of Gethsemane. With the sweat of fear pouring down his brow, he knelt in prayer and begged to be let off the grinding agony that lay in wait for him. But he added the words, 'Father, if it be possible', and, if it should not be possible, then 'Thy will be done'. He accepted that he would have to go through his ordeal to the bitter end, so that the work of redemption could be done. He may have uttered those words — 'thy will be done' — with difficulty, but they meant that he accepted and would be ready to face and to use whatever was in store for him. It was his spoken assurance that he would not run away, that generosity of soul would triumph over fear.

That moment in the Garden has always seemed to me a crucial one, the moment in which Jesus faced up to his own Passion, perhaps in doubt and fear of his own capacity to endure it, but in full acceptance of what had to be. That is a moment we all face at some time or other, when we can opt to run away (to drink? drugs? sexual licence?), to lose ourselves in fantasy or superstition, to submerge ourselves in self-pity; *or*, to look reality in the face, exactly as it is, with all its implications. If we refuse to face reality, we run away from ourselves and turn our backs on the possibility of wholeness. It is no good sinking ourselves in good works: if we are in flight from ourselves, we have nothing to offer other than our own emptiness.

However tempting the flight into unreality may be, there is no lasting comfort in it. Fantasy feeds on itself and turns into madness, drug-taking becomes addiction, drinking easily leads to alcoholism. They are blind alleys. The only cure for suffering is to face it head-on, grasp it round the neck and use it.

Suffering is difficult to define. Basically, it is something (maybe quite minor) which happens against our will, is unpleasant, and blows our carefully-regulated lives asunder. We protest, kicking and screaming for the restoration of the *status quo ante*. If we can persuade ourselves to stop struggling and come to terms with the pain, adapt our natural rhythms to it, accept it as no better and no worse than it is, we may still be floundering in darkness, but the darkness may contain the promise of light. It is a paradox, but one that has been borne out again and again by individual experience, that it is *only* in the darkness, the emptiness and the hopelessness that we find our true selves.

A political prisoner, facing death, once wrote to his fiancée: 'I now realise why man, at certain times of his life, must descend into the depths. First, that he may learn to call upon and cry out to God; second, that he may recognise his own failings; and third, that he may undergo a change of heart.'* C. S. Lewis said the same thing in different words. 'Pain', he wrote, 'is God's megaphone to arouse a deaf world.'† In the normal rush and hullabaloo of life, we have neither time nor mind for personal stock-taking. It is only when we are brought up short, when we are afraid or bewildered or disoriented, that we turn to God with an uncomprehending, frequently agnostic, cry for help. The bubble of our self-esteem has been pricked, our complacency has gone, and we are totally vulnerable. Then and only then can grace begin to operate in us, when we begin to take stock of ourselves, and to listen to our inner voices.

Is it really paradoxical that when we are distressed we turn to the friend who knows what distress can be like? We don't quite know why, but there doesn't seem much point in going for sympathy, the deep-down, understanding kind, to those other friends whose paths have always been smooth. It is as though human beings lack a whole dimension and cannot come to maturity until they have faced sorrow. There is an old Arab proverb which says: 'Too much sunshine makes a desert' and the human heart is very often a desert. But sorrow irrigates the desert. A few years ago a friend of mine, a poet, stricken by the death of a close friend, wrote:

* *Dying We Live*: Collins/Fontana.
† *The Problem of Pain*: C. S. Lewis

Shall I complain
How swift you passed?
Could I regret the widened heart?
Could I complain of it at all?

It is told of Elgar that he once sat and listened admiringly to a young singer with a beautiful voice and faultless technique. She was good, he said, but not great. 'But she will be *great*,' he went on to suggest, 'when something happens to break her heart.' The same holds good for most, if not all, creative artists. There are truths which only sorrow can teach, and it is the source of the most important discoveries about life It is in sorrow that we discover the things which really matter; in sorrow that we discover ourselves. As Ernest Hemingway is said to have written to Scott Fitzgerald, 'When you get the damned hurt use it. Use it and don't cheat.'

When it's our turn to be broken on the wheel, we are aware only of the breaking. The wounds are bleeding and raw, and the pain is so great that it seems impossible to survive it. We are so often beset, not only by the pain of loss or unfulfilled dreams, but by our own personal demons of jealousy or anger or bitterness as well. If we wrestle with the demons we exhaust what little energy we have, and place ourselves even more at their mercy. If any well-meaning fool were to suggest, at such a time, that everything was really for the best, we should be justified in heaving a well-aimed brick. We are not ourselves, our identity is confused, our self-esteem in tatters.

Yet we cannot run away from our own battles without losing ourselves in the process. In the midst of chaos and confusion we catch an occasional glimpse of the calm, still centre of our being, the essence of our true selves, waiting to be discovered,

and the end of our exploring
will be to arrive where we started
and know the place for the first time.*

* *Four Quartets*: T.S. Eliot, Faber and Faber.

If we can stand still and let the storm do its worst, we may still summon the strength to move forward when its bitterest force is spent.

> Blunt the sharpness;
> Untangle the knots,
> Soften the glare.*

The words are from the *Tao Te Ching*, but their meaning is universal. Human beings have a deep need for stillness and harmony. In the standing still, in the acceptance of the unavoidable moment in all its bleakness, lies the possibility of salvation and growth for ourselves and for others. We can say to whatever deity we pray to, 'For what it's worth, here it is. Take it and use it. Use it for the hungry, the homeless, the lonely; for the man down the road who's lost both his job and his wife; for the friend whose little girl has been killed. Use it to help me understand, to be less self-centred, more loving.'

Heaven knows, we may be feeling so wretched that we have to do violence to ourselves to utter such a prayer. We may do so through clenched teeth. But if we even hope one day to mean what we say, we are expressing a trust that one day, though not yet, all will again be well; and all will finally be well. On that day we shall at last 'arrive where we started' and know what it is to be whole.

* *Tao Te Ching*: Lao Tzu, Penguin Classics.